Eustace Clare Grenville Murray

The Member for Paris

A tale of the Second Empire. Vol. 2

Eustace Clare Grenville Murray

The Member for Paris
A tale of the Second Empire. Vol. 2

ISBN/EAN: 9783337245481

Printed in Europe, USA, Canada, Australia, Japan

Cover: Foto ©ninafisch / pixelio.de

More available books at **www.hansebooks.com**

THE MEMBER FOR PARIS:

A TALE OF THE SECOND EMPIRE.

BY

TROIS-ETOILES.

"A force de marcher l'homme erre, l'esprit doute,
Tous laissent quelquechose aux buissons de la route,
Les troupeaux leur toison et l'homme sa vertu."—Victor Hugo.

IN THREE VOLUMES.

VOL. II.

LONDON:
SMITH, ELDER & CO., 15, WATERLOO PLACE.
1871.

CONTENTS.

CHAP.		PAGE
I.	LOVE AND WAR	1
II.	M. MACROBE OFFERS MONEY	31
III.	M. POCHEMOLLE'S REQUEST	48
IV.	M. MACROBE INSERTS THE THIN END OF THE WEDGE	68
V.	HOW EMPIRES ARE GOVERNED	92
VI.	MADEMOISELLE ANGÉLIQUE	120
VII.	"THE FUTURE MADAME FILOSELLE"	139
VIII.	M. MACROBE "AT HOME"	152
IX.	YOUNG CANDOUR, OLD SUBTLETY	173
X.	"LE LION AMOUREUX"	200
XI.	CANVASSING	211
XII.	VOX POPULI	234
XIII.	MACROBE À LA RESCOUSSE	254
XIV.	EPISTOLARY	284
XV.	A SPEECH, A VOTE, AND A SURPRISE	300
XVI.	A RECOGNITION	325

THE MEMBER FOR PARIS.

CHAPTER I.

LOVE AND WAR.

No, Georgette had not been well lately, and the excellent M. Pochemolle, his wife, and even M. Alcibiade Pochemolle, had been growing a little uneasy at seeing that the blooming young girl, once so gladsome, had become by degrees unaccountably subdued and pensive. They questioned her as to whether she felt unwell, but she replied that she had no consciousness of being otherwise than usual—that there was nothing the matter.

And yet matter there was, though probably Georgette was sincere enough in asserting that she was not conscious of it. Several weeks had elapsed since the present of the work-box by Horace Gerold. She had hemmed him the cambric bands; then, fearing that the gift would not be complete, she had wished to add a dozen handkerchiefs, and this had taken time—it takes time to work twelve times over the letters H.G., when there are so many pauses for reverie between the stitches. And during the weeks that she had slowly plied her needle in marking the cambric with the two initials, she had seen Horace pass the window every morning and lift his hat and smile to her as he went on his way to the newspaper-office; and she had heard of his having entered journalism and of his new triumphs in that profession. Out of compliment to his lodger, and although he indignantly repudiated the doctrines advocated in that print, M. Pochemolle had made it a point to subscribe to the *Sentinelle*, and in the evening, when she retired to her room, Georgette took the paper with her and would sit up in her bed reading the articles by Horace. She did not always understand them at first, but she would read them over and over until she did; and if she was not successful after many readings, then she would read the signature a multitude of times, and that pleased her: she fancied, somehow, the letters were in his own handwriting. When she had read the papers she put them all carefully by in a drawer. M. Alcibiade Pochemolle sometimes wondered what became of them.

She no longer carried up their letters to the brothers when they were brought to the wrong door. There is an instinct in these things. But she would gaze with curious scrutiny at the envelopes directed in feminine hands. When there were none such she was happier.

She had noticed, with the quick eye of a woman for such trifles, that Horace Gerold was turning fashionable. He had an eyeglass, wore light-coloured gloves and lacquered boots, smoked cigars instead of the cigarettes which he used to twirl himself, and always came home at night in cabs. She could hear the vehicles stop in the street outside, and then his step as he mounted the staircase. She never went to sleep until she heard that step—not if it were delayed till four o'clock in the morning. One day, Horace had come into the shop and brought them a private box for the opera—she had once remarked in his presence that she loved music. The performance was *Robert le Diable*. Nothing could have been more hospitable or more full of tact than the arrangements made by him for their comfort. He had chartered a private brougham to convey and bring them back; and in the second entr'acte had paid them a visit in their box, bringing two bouquets, one for herself and one for her mother, and a fine *cornet* of bonbons, without which the happiness of a Parisian *bourgeoise* at the "playhouse" is never complete. Upon the drawing up of the curtain he had discreetly taken his leave. It had been a great evening for everybody. M. Alcibiade Pochemolle had never put on so much bear's-grease in the course of his existence, and the sight of the *corps-de-ballet* made his fingers tingle; M. Pochemolle had reckoned that there were at least a hundred square yards of canvas in the drop-scene; Madame Pochemolle had been much impressed by the resurrection of the ghost-nuns in the churchyard scene. As for Georgette, she had remarked but one thing, and that was, that Horace on returning to his stall had bowed to several stately and beautiful ladies in the boxes, and that at the close of the third act he had appeared in the box of one covered with diamonds, whom M. Pochemolle had recognized for a Marchioness of the Noble Faubourg. Alone in her room after the opera, and with her bouquet in her hand, the poor child shivered mournfully. Who was she that she could hope to vie with ladies who wore diamonds and were Marchionesses? It was evident M. Gerold had never given her a thought.

Nevertheless, she had moments of flitting compensation; and her cheeks mantled on the morrow of the day when Horace had found her present on his table and came down to thank her with his bright voice, which seemed to her more refined and gentle each time she heard it. He drew out one of the handkerchiefs, which was lightly scented with mignonette, admired the embroidery of the initials—indeed no common piece of workmanship—and playfully observed he intended keeping this fine linen for great occasions: "My wedding-day, for instance," said he, "providing I ever do marry." And at these words she turned pale anew; it was like a cloud passing rapidly over a furtive sunbeam.

The probabilities are that Horace did not remark this pallor, though he could not help noticing in a general way that she was changed since he had spoken with her last. He told her how sorry he was to hear she had been unwell, and drew forth the rather faltering answer that, indeed, she felt in perfect health.

This time he was struck with the tone of the reply, and it recurred to him at intervals in the course of the day, and again once or twice during the week when passing by the shop he remarked that Georgette's eyes lowered under his with a new expression which he did not understand. Then this circumstance faded out of his mind under the pressure of graver preoccupations which soon beset him.

He underwent the common lot of Parisian journalists, and got engaged in a quarrel with a brother pen-man in the opposite camp. The fault was not his, nor altogether his adversary's, but that of the admirable political system under which they both lived. The conditions of the French Press were then such that journalists could not well help coming to loggerheads try as they might. The unlucky law Tinguy-Laboulie (named after the two old gentlemen who promoted it), which rendered it binding upon the writer of an article to sign his name to it, had completely disorganized the old anonymous Press by substituting individualism for combined action and conflict of personalities for polemic of opinions. The staff of a newspaper was no longer a disciplined company, but a band of sharp-shooters, each of the members of which, being personally responsible for the opinions he emitted, naturally did his utmost to assert himself. Had the Press been free, the discussions between man and man need not necessarily have degenerated into violence, for it is not the tendency of educated men to abuse one another when they have fair arguments at their command. But, hemmed in as journalists were on every side by penal clauses, which made it impossible to write on any subject with latitude, the temptation to glide from trammelled controversy into exchange of personal invectives was often irresistible. Opposition writers would break out into vituperation, as a train will jump off the line because obstacles are set in the way of its straight course; but more frequently the aggressors were the members of the semi-official Press. These gentlemen, being obliged to defend the acts of their Government, by hook or by crook, might have found the task an up-hill one had the only weapons allowed them been those of logic; but matters were much simplified when they could champion Imperial policy with a pen in one hand and a foil in the other. If the pen found nothing to say, the foil came to the rescue, and it was not an unusual thing to attempt silencing troublesome writers in the liberal ranks by picking a series of bones with them, until they either held their peace, overawed, or retaliated by spitting a few of their antagonists one after the other. This was what was tried with Horace.

There was an Imperialist paper named *Le Pavois* and on the staff of it one M. Paul de Cosaque, a Creole, with a frizzly head of hair, large round eyes, and hands like small shoulders of mutton. This promising youth, though not above five-and-twenty, was the Quixote of his party, serving the dynasty in a devoted Creole way, and hating oppositionists as a tough young bull-dog might vermin. He was not long in taking offence at the successes of Horace. Hearing his name so constantly mentioned, he ended by growing tired of it, and did not conceal his longing for an opportunity of coming into collision with one whose popularity he was pleased to regard as in some sort a personal affront to himself. So he proceeded to do what is called in journalistic phrase "laying a man on the gridiron," which means that he collared Horace Gerold and served him up every day to the readers of the *Parois*, skewered through and through with an epigram. They were somewhat blunt, these epigrams of M. Paul de Cosaque, but the intention of them was plain enough, and, at the outset, Horace was for despatching a couple of seconds to request that satisfaction might be afforded him. But, with a shrug, Nestor Roche poohpoohed this notion, saying it were best to take no heed of the barking of a cur; so that M. Paul, perceiving a reluctance to quarrel, set down his adversary for a chicken-heart, and began unwisely to crow cock-a-whoop before the time.

Now one day, after this fleabiting had been going on for some weeks, Horace wrote a leader in the *Sentinelle* on the subject of the privacy of the parliamentary debates. It was a very temperate article though, not without a dash of acid, and it had been ably revised by Nestor Roche, who had given it the backbone it at first wanted. Several foreign papers, and most of the liberal provincial organs, quoted it; and as the law which debarred the public from knowing what went on in their own Parliament was an ever-chafing sore, the author received a good many congratulations from Boulevard politicians. This was just the sort of occasion M. Paul de Cosaque had been looking for. He was down on the article in a trice, dipping his pen in his smartest verjuice, and howling out abuse much as a faithful negro might do who had seen his master's shins scraped. Horace was on a visit to his editor at the prison of Ste. Pélagie when the number of the *Pavois* containing M. Paul's attack fell into his hands. Nestor Roche, Max Delormay, and another captive journalist named Jean Kerjou of the *Gazette des Boulevards*, were sitting at the table writing. The printer's devil, Trigger, who had just brought all the morning papers in a vast bundle under his arm, was planted on a chair, whence his legs dangled, and his one eye squinted, waiting for "copy." Horace himself was lounging on the ottoman and smoking as he read.

He started up with the colour rising to his face and an indignant glare in his eyes.

"Look at this, M. Roche," he said, and began to stride about the room, biting his lips. "It is time this should end now. I shall send the fellow my seconds this afternoon."

"No; wait till to-morrow," put in Jean Kerjou. "I shall be out of prison then, and I'll act for you. Who is the man?"

Nestor Roche ran his quick glance through the column and presently answered: "Well, my boy, it's one of the necessities of our trade to fight as well as scribble. This whelp's trying to draw you; you must break his teeth. But, first, we'll just give him a rap with his own weapons and make his copper-coloured knuckles ring."

The four journalists were soon in consultation round the board with the open number of the *Pavois* before them. What they wanted was to draw up a retort which should strike at the weak place in M. Paul's armour, and make that sword-clinker yell. This weak place was not difficult to find. M. Paul, like many other worthy people, was not above the foible of vanity, and had tacked on to his patronymic a name which did not lawfully belong to him. His real style and title was Paul Panier; but Panier being an ugly name, signifying "basket," he, or rather he and his father between them, had discarded it in favour of the more sounding designation De Cosaque, which was derived from the country residence of the elder Panier. But these usurpations are formally prohibited by law under pain of imprisonment; and it was, therefore, very much like throwing projectiles out of a glass-house when M. Paul delivered himself as follows in his attack upon Horace:—

". . . . As for these so-called Republicans, who go about under false names, being ashamed to wear the titles which their fathers bore lest they should compromise their popularity with the rabble; as for these self-styled Democrats, who refuse homage to a king, but fawn sycophantly upon the mob, and see no better way of currying favour with their masters than by making litter of all the distinctions their own ancestors won, just like those low birds who befoul their own nests;—as for these men, we know what is their object in asking that the debates of the Chamber may again be thrown open to public audiences. They have not forgotten 1793, when the galleries were filled with drunken trollops, whose bloodthirsty howls gave our precious Republicans the courage they needed to send old men, women, and fallen kings to the scaffold; nor 1848, when the scum of our galleys infested the Strangers' tribunes to cheer the dismal buffooneries of such men as the citizen Manuel Gerold. We should not wonder if those who ask that the tribunes may be thrown open again, had an eye to some day becoming deputies themselves; but, being aware of the contempt with which their utterances would be received by men of sense, they wish to make sure of having an audience of kindred spirits—like those tenth-rate actors who, unable to excite applause in the stalls and boxes, pick some poor devils out of the gutter and hire them for five sous a night to go and clap their hands in the pit."

There was nothing uncommon in the form of this effusion; it was the true semi-official style of the period.

Nestor Roche prepared the following reply, which Horace signed :—

" *The* Marquis of Clairefontaine *to* M. Paul
" Panier.

" The gentleman on the staff of the *Pavois* who calls himself M. 'de Cosaque,' is respectfully informed that the undersigned writer will resume the title he inherited from his ancestors on the day his courteous antagonist does likewise. M. Paul 'de Cosaque' will doubtless see fit to perform this resumption without delay, lest the Public Prosecutor, forgetting that M. 'de Cosaque' is a Bonapartist, and remembering only that he is a transgressor of the law, which forbids persons to adopt nobiliary particles to which they have no right, should order his transfer to Mazas, and so afford him the opportunity of making a closer acquaintance with those 'scum of the galleys,' with whose language, as well as with whose habits, M. 'de Cosaque' appears so conversant.

"Horace Gerold."

This again was a very fair specimen of an Opposition retort.

"This will save you the trouble of sending a challenge," remarked the editor. "The whelp will probably begin operations himself;" and he handed the slip to Trigger, who, after receiving his usual instruction not to loiter with fellow *gamins*, shambled off with it to the printing-office.

The effect, however, was not quite what Nestor Roche and his acolytes expected. On reading the stinging paragraph M. Paul de Cosaque blanched, but he did not set out in quest of seconds. He caught up his hat and went off prowling in the direction of the Boulevards, grinding his white creole teeth and clenching his fists so tight that the nails left four dents in each of the brown palms. He wanted to find Horace and knock him down; then fight him with steel afterwards. There is no profession like literature for making a man mild and brotherly.

Horace was breakfasting at one of the great restaurants, and with him, as it chanced, was Jean Kerjou, the man of the *Gazette des Boulevards*, who had been released from confinement in the morning. He was a Breton, this journalist, short, but thick and powerful, and amazingly prompt with his hands, like all Bretons. He had taken a fancy to Horace, who knew but little of him, and the pair were, so to say, watering their new-sprung friendship in this breakfast.

Suddenly Jean Kerjou, who sat opposite the door, dissecting a woodcock, abandoned his bird, crying, "Haro, Gerold, look out!" and sprang to his legs. The mulatto face of M. Paul was darkening the doorway, and in less than two seconds was within blow-reach of them.

M. Paul held a newspaper crunched up in his right hand. He strode up to the table, jabbered something unintelligible, and, before any one in the crowded restaurant could stop him, delivered a tremendous cuff, which missed Horace's head by an ace, alighted, with a loud thwack, on the countenance of a waiter, and sent him sprawling on to a table where lunched a peaceful English family, who set up piercing cries.

There was an inconceivable uproar, amidst

which a huge slap resounded, and simultaneously an unholy crash of broken glass, as some one not distinguishable was hurled, all of a lump, into a corner. The slap was administered by Horace: the crash was caused by Jean Kerjou, who had caught up M. Paul like a bundle of linen, and shot him to the other end of the room.

Twenty arms at once pinned down the creole, gnashing and struggling to rise; twenty others pulled back Horace Gerold and Jean Kerjou, to prevent further mischief. Then uprose a deafening contestation as to who was the aggressor—the English family shrieking all together that it was the negro, and the waiter thundering that it was Horace, seeing that, had the blow fallen on his cheek as it was meant to do, half the disturbance would have been avoided. In the midst of the hubbub entered two policemen, who took down the names of everybody all round, apprehended the waiter on the ground that, being splashed all over with lobster-sauce, he was presumably the culprit; and, on being eventually induced to release him, retired bewildered, leaving the field clear to a gentleman with a countenance like a weasel's, who, having been witness of the whole scene, stepped forward, with his mouth full, and spluttered, "I maintain, it's an act of the most brutal aggression. M. Paul de Cosaque, you've conducted yourself like a villain. Do you hear that?"

There was no mistaking this twanging voice. It was M. Macrobe's. He had been lunching with a stock-broking friend, and this friend, fearful that he would get himself into trouble, now sought to restrain him by the coat-tails; but M. Macrobe would not be restrained. He rushed up to the infuriated creole, who was with difficulty kept from flying at his throat, and shouted, "Men like yourself are a disgrace to the Press, M. Panier. You convert what should be the noblest of professions into a bravo's trade. You deserve to be stamped out like a pestilent toad, and if M. Gerold doesn't kill you, I will."

M. Paul de Cosaque was forcibly dragged

out of the restaurant. M. Macrobe turned, apparently trembling with the holiest indignation and sympathy, and walked to where Horace and his friend were standing. The least Horace Gerold could do for a man who had taken his part so warmly was to thank him, which he did at once and with gratitude, though coldly. M. Macrobe, not minding the coldness, continued to strike whilst the iron was hot.

"My dear young friend," said he, "that man is a very cut-throat. He has had half-a-dozen men out already, and will nip your brilliant career short if we let him; but trust to me: I will be your second. It was he who first raised his hand on you. This makes you the offended party, and gives you choice of weapons."

Horace did not much relish the proposal of M. Macrobe to be his second; but to refuse would, under the circumstances, have been both discourteous and ungracious. Besides, Jean Kerjou did not leave him time to do so, for, delighted with the pluck of "the small man with the ferret face," he held out his hand,

and said, "Sir, my name is Jean Kerjou, and I am M. Gerold's other second. Between us we will see our friend well through this scrape."

Further breakfast being impossible, Horace threw down five napoleons to the landlord to pay for the breakages, and two more to the waiter to soothe his throbbing jaw. Then he, Jean Kerjou, and the banker, slipped out by a back door to escape the mob, which had already congregated outside, wide-mouthed, and so home to Horace's lodgings. The two policemen, before retiring, had suggested that everybody should call upon the Commissary of Police during the afternoon to explain matters; but this formality was omitted, for the police official could neither have undone that which was accomplished nor prevented that which was to come. In the course of a couple of hours Jean Kerjou and M. Macrobe had routed out Emile from a musty court, in which he was acting as junior in a fearfully musty case, and hastily apprised him of what had happened: after which they had called upon M. de Cosaque, and arranged a rendezvous with the latter's two friends at five. By dinner-time the duel was all settled. It was to come off at seven the next morning, in the Bois de Vincennes, with foils.

Of course the news spread quickly along the Boulevards, and was received with no inconsiderable glee by the do-nothing portion of the public. These tiffs between journalists were the one thing that saved the press of the period from monotony, and a duel was always a welcome little episode. All the evening papers gave accounts of the fracas at the restaurant; but, in order not to spoil sport, *i.e.* bring the police on the ground, they fraternally abstained from divulging the spot where the fight was to take place. Nevertheless, they printed the names of the contending parties in full, with those of their seconds, and hinted significantly that M. Paul de Cosaque was one of the best swordsmen in Paris.

By the advice of his two friends, who took bodily charge of him during the evening, Horace dined lightly, and gave an hour to fencing, in which he was already tolerably proficient. At half-past nine he was escorted to his door, with injunctions to go to bed as soon as possible, and be up by six the next day.

The day might be called an eventful one, but he mounted his staircase with a very quiet pulse for a man who was going to risk his life at sunrise.

Just as he reached the *entresol*, however, a door was timidly held ajar, and he was confronted by Georgette.

She had read of the impending duel in the newspaper, and ever since her mind had been distracted by visions of blood and death. She was pale and terrified, and held the newspaper in her hands. When she saw Horace she said nothing, but shed a few tears.

He was touched by this unexpected meeting, and by the simple display of grief, of which he could not but guess the cause.

"Why are you crying, Mademoiselle Georgette?" he said, gently.

She made no answer, but pointed to the paragraph in the newspaper.

He took one of her unresisting hands in his, and said with gaiety, "But there is nothing to be afraid of in that. Duels happen every day."

"You may be killed," she sobbed.

"And if I were, would you grieve for me?" he asked, half in jest, half gravely.

She threw him a sad, reproachful look.

"Don't speak like that, Monsieur Horace; you know how unhappy I—how unhappy we should all be," added she, correcting herself.

He took her other hand, looked into her eyes, and said, "I shall run no danger, Georgette."

This was the first time he called her Georgette. She strove gently to free herself: but the effort was short-lived.

"Promise me you won't fight to-morrow," she faltered.

"I promise you he shall not hurt me, Georgette," he answered, encircling her waist with his arm.

"Oh, but if he should——" she said, making another feeble attempt to disengage herself.

"But he won't, Georgette."

And, stooping, he pressed a kiss on her lips.

But theirs was the bliss of a few instants only, for at that moment the house-door opened, then closed, and the steps of a lodger in the vestibule below warned them to separate.

"Good-night, Georgette," he whispered. "I shall be safe to-morrow if you return me my kiss. It will be my talisman."

He was still holding her waist. She blushed; looked over the balusters to see if the lodger was coming, and then returned him his kiss.

* * * * *

The next morning betimes, one of the keepers of the Bois de Vincennes, returning to his cottage from night-duty, beheld two broughams, following each other at an interval of a few minutes, sweep along the road to the race-course and stop near a secluded knoll, distant some couple of hundred yards from the Grand Stand; and, being a man of experience, he knew what that meant. Chancing to be further a shrewd man, he resolved upon retracing his steps, and, instead of going home, to take up his position at a distance, though within eye-view, so as to be ready to come forward when everything was over and earn an honest twenty-franc piece, by undertaking to preserve secrecy. To these ends he ensconced himself behind the trunks of some felled trees.

M. Macrobe, who had managed matters for Horace, had done everything very well. He had brought his brougham, with store of lint, bandages, restoratives, &c. concealed in the pockets; the most eminent surgeon in Paris on one of the front seats; and a pair of the finest duelling-foils in a chamois bag. He had quite won the graces of Jean Kerjou, both by his energy, his practical hints, and the loud-spoken sympathy he evinced for Horace. In sooth, M. Macrobe had been somewhat gloomy the preceding afternoon, on his principal insisting upon fighting with foils; and his gloom had not cleared up until he had seen how Horace bore himself in the fencing school. Horace, though he never boasted of it, and never sought to air his talent, was a good fencer; having been originally taught by his father, who, first as a nobleman, then as an officer, and finally as a journalist, had served a treble apprenticeship in sword-craft. M. Macrobe was elated to see the manner in which he could parry and lunge, and though he would still have preferred pistols, on the ground that a man with steady nerves can blow his adversary out of life with this weapon, and not allow time to be shot at in return, yet he felt considerably reassured as to his principal's prospects even against such an antagonist as M. de Cosaque.

Horace Gerold's party were the first on the ground. Upon the others appearing, the eight gentlemen all bowed together, but there were no negotiations attempted—the insults exchanged being such as could only be washed out by bloodshed. The two seconds of M. de Cosaque— one a colonel of the Imperial Guard and a man of the *coup-d'état,* the other, M. de Gargousse, an official deputy—selected the ground along with MM. Macrobe and Kerjou, and then examined the different pairs of foils that had been brought. By common consent those of M. Macrobe were chosen;

they were very ribbons of steel that could be bent so that the point touched the handle without snapping. Whilst these preliminaries were being adjusted, the two principals took off their coats, waistcoats, hats, cravats, and boots—so as not to slip on the wet morning grass;—and opened their shirts a little, as etiquette required, to show that they wore no mail-coat next the skin. Meantime, the two surgeons, standing aside and conversing in a low voice, fumbled in their pockets to open their surgical cases, in order that no time might be lost when their cheerful services were needed. The morning was deliciously balmy; and in the wood could be heard the tinkling of a cart-bell, and the lively voice of the carter speaking to his horse as they jogged together to their work. It is only human beings who could think of fighting on such a morning as that.

There was a silence. The combatants were face to face, two yards apart. The Colonel having measured the foils, gave one to each, then joined the two weapons by the points, and, stepping back

with head uncovered, said, "Allez, Messieurs."—
Then the guard ensconced behind the fallen trees
saw this:—

The strongest of the two duellists, he with the
dark face and large hands, bore down upon his
adversary with a terrific onslaught, forcing him
to "break" and parry wildly; then, when it
seemed as though the quickness of the retreat
must cause the slighter combatant to lose his
balance, the other made a rapid, furious lunge.
The attack was so formidable that any but a first-
rate fencer would have been carried off his legs by
it. The guard — an old soldier—winced. But
the slighter man rallied with desperate strength,
struck up the sword that was within a hair's-
breadth of his heart, plunged forward, and with
the suddenness of lightning thrust his foil through
his adversary's chest up to the hilt. The whole
thing did not last fifty seconds. M. Paul de
Cosaque rolled over on the grass, with the foil
still in him, quite dead.

Four out of the seven spectators turned pale.

The Colonel glanced at Horace and saluted him with respect. M. Macrobe pressed up and wrung his hand. The guard loomed from behind his trees and came up slowly, in pursuit of his twenty francs.

CHAPTER II.

M. MACROBE OFFERS MONEY.

The lucky hazard that had thrown M. Macrobe in the way of Horace at the restaurant, had gratified one of that sagacious financier's most deep-rooted wishes. A few days before, talking with M. Louchard the Commissary of Police, with whom, as with a good many strange persons, he was on affable terms, the latter had said to him: "By the way, M. Macrobe, do you know that the young radical who spoke against you in the libel-suit is by birth a marquis, and owns vast wealth?"

"Yes, I know it," responded M. Macrobe curiously; "but how did *you* know it?"

"Why, after the trial, seeing that the popularity of this young man threatened to become a danger to public order, the Prefect sent me to search his apartments." Here M. Louchard lowered his voice, for they were in a public place, and gave an account of his domiciliary visit to the brothers' lodgings, omitting that episode, however, which related to the threat of Horace to break his head. "And, odd to say," he concluded, "we found a deed by which the old Republican, Manuel Gerold, makes over to his two sons the whole of the estates of Hautbourg during his own lifetime."

M. Macrobe pricked up his ears.

"Have you that deed still in your possession, M. Louchard?"

"Why, yes," answered the commissary, glad to interest the powerful financier. "I took it to the Prefect, who read it, but ordered me to return it, the document being a family paper of no use to us. I should have done so ere now, but forgot. However, this deed has not been so useless as M. le Préfet pretends: for it has proved to us that these two young Gerolds are an extremely suspicious pair. Having wealth, they yet live as if they had nothing, which is evidence enough that they must lay out their money to unlawful ends. We suspect they are subsidizing secret societies, and we have got them under close supervision."

"Oh, they are under police surveillance?"

"The very closest. We have men watching them day and night. There is not a thing they do but we know of it."

"Yet, I'll be bound you don't know who they bank with, though this piece of knowledge might have stood you in better stead than many others which I daresay you've picked up." And M. Macrobe looked rather sarcastically at the man of Police.

"No, we've not found who they bank with," answered M. Louchard reflectively. "And I suppose *you* can't tell us."

"They bank with us," replied M. Macrobe carelessly; "but I can't tell you anything as to where their money goes. The revenue of the estates is paid into our hands every quarter-day by the agent; but it is drawn out again almost as soon by this same agent with cheques signed by old M. Gerold. That's all we know about it."

Then turning pensive, he added, " You will show me that deed, M. Louchard."

"Willingly," rejoined the other, who counted that his civility would be repaid by financial hints; since none knew better than M. Macrobe how to give hints as to securities worth dabbling in, and shares which, though prosperous in aspect, had best be avoided. Everybody gambled on the Bourse in those days of jobbing, and M. Louchard did like the rest. But it was not every one who had such a master tipster as M. Macrobe to guide him.

The two went together to M. Louchard's office, and the banker had a sight of the deed of gift, which he scrutinized long and narrowly. In return for the favour he thus advised M. Louchard:— " The shares of the Crédit Parisien are quoted to-day at 850. I'll let you have twenty of them at 800. You shall pay me in a month. Hold fast to them till they're quoted at 1,500, which they will be in less than a couple of years, and then sell out." M. Louchard almost went down on all fours, thanking him with transports as a benefactor.

The deed of gift set M. Macrobe thinking. He

was an astute man, and soon put his thoughts into plain figures. So long as he had imagined that Horace Gerold would have to await his father's death before stepping into the Hautbourg estate, he had treated the angling of him as a thing that could be undertaken leisurely; but now that Horace was actually master of his property, he was a fish to bait and hook with the least delay possible. M. Macrobe had reached that pitch of wealth where gold comes flowing in like a Pactolus, on the immutable principle by which rivers always roll their waters towards the sea, which has enough without them. But his were paper riches. They were the riches that give a man consideration on 'Change, make his name familiar among brokers, and cause the outside public to speak of him as a warm man. M. Macrobe, however, desired something more than this. With opulence had come the ambition which opulence begets. The enriched stock-jobber longed to be somebody, and the surest way to become somebody is to be at the head of an ancient name and a substantial landed estate—

neither of which essentials M. Macrobe possessed. Under the circumstances, it was not very surprising that a man, accustomed like him to put things in black and white, should think of his daughter and propose making her minister to his honest ambition. If she should marry a nobleman with influence at his command, that influence would naturally be at the service of her father, and give him a lift into that political world, where M. Macrobe now longed to try his powers. He turned over this thought maturely and in an infinite variety of lights, but always with the same result, to wit, that Horace Gerold and his daughter Angélique were evidently made for one another.

With M. Macrobe to plan was to resolve. Obstacles did not daunt him. He had surmounted so many already to make himself what he was, that the aversion which the two Gerolds testified towards him struck him as a mere vexatious circumstance—nothing more. That he should finally overcome the ill-feeling, he did not for a moment doubt; and he set himself to the concoction of sundry diplomatic schemes, by which he and Horace were to be brought together. But the merit of these schemes he never had the need to test, for as we have seen, hazard suddenly played his cards for him, and did more in a day than he, by his wits unaided, could have done in a twelvemonth.

After the duel Horace was bound to him by one of those ties which men of honour regard as strong. He had espoused the young man's quarrel openly and fearlessly in public, thus risking his life for him—there being no question that, had M. Paul de Cosaque triumphed, he would have visited M. Macrobe's interference in such a way as to lay that gentleman and his schemes of glory six good feet under ground. Horace might regret not having acted with more caution in accepting M. Macrobe's friendly offices; but it was too late for repentance now. He was under an obligation to the financier, and the latter determined, by a skilful stroke, to put all that remained of his antipathy to flight.

It had been somewhat of a shock to Nestor

Roche, when he heard that his young ally had gone out to fight, with the slippery stock-jobber for his second; and though, upon Horace rushing into the prison-room a couple of hours after the duel, the joy at beholding him safe was such as, for the moment, to dispel all other pre-occupations, yet by-and-by, when the old editor had had time to grow calm and gruff again, he said, with a shade of pain, "I could have wished to see you with a worthier henchman on the field, my boy."

"I could have wished to have had you," replied Horace, gravely; "but I owe a debt to M. Macrobe."

And he proceeded to relate what had occurred, being backed in his narrative by Jean Kerjou, who spoke of the financier as having behaved throughout "like a trump." This did not convert Nestor Roche, but it appeased him, though soon his brow grew dark again when Horace said, a little timidly, "And, do you know, I have a message from this very M. Macrobe to you, M. Roche?"

"To me!" exclaimed the editor, impassively.

"Well, yes. This morning, after the duel, M. Kerjou, here present, and I breakfasted with him, and he fell to talking about the libel-trial. He was very frank, but full of tact about it. He said we must not bear him a grudge for having defended his good name, but that he sought to make no profit out of the action, and that he hoped you would take back the five-and-twenty thousand francs damages the court had made you pay."

Here Horace drew out a pocket-book.

Nestor Roche frowned.

"You needn't offer me that man's money. If he is lucky enough to persuade you that he is an injured man, I have nothing to say; but you know my opinion of him. I've not changed it."

"Yet it seems to me this should induce us to mitigate our judgment," observed Horace, sticking up for the man who had stood by him. "After all, I duresay he's no worse than thousands of others we call honest men; and here he has sent you back your twenty-five thousand francs, which is a great deal more than many others would have done."

Nestor Roche eyed him rather compassionately, and answered with dryness:—

"My boy, men will always get the weather-side of you with smooth tongues. Think well of this stock-jobber if you like, but take him back his money."

And he would hear not a word more on the subject.

Horace felt hurt at this shortness, and so did Jean Kerjou a little, for it did not suit this straightforward Breton to suppose that he had been shaking hands with a man who had any taint on him. He said so frankly, and was putting it with some earnestness to Nestor Roche whether the latter had anything definite to allege against the banker Macrobe, when Max Delormay, the editor Tirecruchon, and a number of other political captives, tumbled in, attracted by the report of Horace Gerold's presence.

Much hand-shaking ensued, as well as congratulations on the issue of the duel; but of pity for the fallen man not a word. To be sure, M. de

Cosaque was not a personage in whose favour one could get up much sympathy. He had been as a Goliath in the midst of his party, overshadowing his foes with his shoulder-of-mutton fist, slapping their faces on slender pretexts, and transfixing them afterwards without remorse. To have wished him alive would have been to wish an ever-threatening foil over one's head.

"A more bloodthirsty dog I never set eyes on," ejaculated the fat M. de Tirecruchon, with a sigh of relief. "Egad! he had *me* out once. Happily, it was with pistols, but he blew half the rim of my hat away."

"*De mortuis*——" began honest Jean Kerjou. He had not yet got over the tragic episode of the morning.

Soon the room was hazy with tobacco-smoke, and a dozen prisoners lay or sat recumbent on sofa, arm-chairs, and ottoman; Horace forming the centre of the group, seated on a low stool, and being made much of by the rest. Still a little sore at Nestor Roche's strictures upon M. Macrobe, he was rather moody and silent, and hoped the financier and his offer would be allowed to drop for a while, until he could be alone with Nestor Roche, and talk the point over with him. But Jean Kerjou, who was uneasy, and wanted to get his mind clear, made haste to resume his interrupted appeal to the editor, and so drew on a general discussion concerning M. Macrobe's proposal to refund the damages. The case was quite a novel one, and tolerably difficult to pronounce upon impartially. Opinions were pretty equally divided.

M. de Tirecruchon, who was nothing if not indulgent of everybody's foibles, his own included, held stoutly with the Macrobians.

"Corbleu!" he exclaimed, rolling one of his flat *panatellas* between two thick fingers, and glancing at his editorial brother with surprise— "Corbleu! Roche, you're not going to refuse such an offer as that? Of course Macrobe is more or less of a rogue, but aren't we all rogues, present company excepted? I wouldn't give a fig for a man who wasn't something of a rogue. Besides, don't you see that the more you've got to say against the man, so much the greater is the reason for taking his money. If what you said against him was true, *ergo* it was no slander: consequently, the damages were unjustly assessed, and, therefore, obviously, you have a right to repocket them."

Horace bridled up.

"I didn't wish to see the matter viewed in that light; I would rather the offer were accepted generously, as it was made, and that we should acknowledge, some of us, that we may have been a little hasty in judging M. Macrobe."

"Yes, so should I," assented Jean Kerjou, candidly;—"or, at least," added he, "I should like to hear something plain and proveable against this man."

M. Max Delormay here felt it due to himself to protest energetically. The famous paragraph he had written against M. Macrobe, and for which he, as well as others, were suffering fines and imprisonment, had gradually come to assume in his eyes the proportion of an historical event. He was not very remote from the idea that since this paragraph the financier had become somehow his own peculiar private property, and that to speak of him in any way, either *pro* or *con*, without his, Max Delormay's, sanction, was to defraud him, Max Delormay, of his just privileges. Accordingly, he claimed his right to protest, and, in that sober tone which Frenchmen have when they don't know what they are saying, made a speech which nobody understood, he least of all; but which concluded with a panegyric of the Spartan Republic as being a place where commercial morality flourished.

M. de Tirecruchon puffed his jovial face with an air of bewilderment, and cried: " Tut, Max, you're running off with the wrong bone. The question is, whether Roche shall accept back 25,000 francs paid by him as damages for an article you wrote. I say yes; and I've given you my reasons. As for morality nowadays, I'll tell you what it just amounts to—not being found out. Go you into the streets and take at haphazard out of our church-folk, politicians, tradesmen, or out of us journalists, any hundred men, and I will be bound there are not two out of the lot whose lives will bear looking into with a microscope. Hang it all! let us not get to prying too closely behind each other's curtains. I don't know who this Macrobe is. In times past he may have been a coiner, for all I can tell; but at present the Government accepts him, the Law accepts him, and Society accepts him, so why shouldn't I? For come! what would it profit me, if, after making the acquaintance of the man, finding him pleasant, sensible, ready to do one a good turn, &c., I were to go and rake up the diary of his life, to see if I could discover one soiled page in it? To-morrow the fellow might die; and what should I have gained by my trouble then?—not even the pleasure of cutting him. Much better seek to know nothing about the soiled page, and take the fellow's hand so long as I find it agreeable. Of course if I receive proof positive that the fellow is a cur, that's another question; but I haven't.'

A small, dark man, squatting near the fire and smoking a clay pipe, whom Horace knew as the Citizen Albi, a political conspirator, who unaffectedly admired Robespierre, and was of opinion that the Reign of Terror had failed in its effects from not being quite stringent enough, here broke in vehemently:

"Your views are as immoral as they well can be. If adopted they would be the charter of successful rogues. When you are hiring a servant you rake up all you can about him, and if you find a speck you draw back. I see no difference between rich rogues and poor. I have never yet given my hand to a man whose life was not as clear to me as the noon-day, and, so help me my own contempt for scoundrels, I never will."

"And what is the result, my poor Albi?" rejoined the stout editor, unruffled. "Why, ever since you could hold a musket you have been in open war with Society. Out of your short life of thirty years you have spent eight in transportations or imprisonments: and I daresay if I could read in your heart I should find smouldering there the scheme of some new communistical era of guillotining, by which you hope to regenerate us. Those are gloomy principles, my poor friend, which make you thirst for our blood so ardently, and oblige Society in its own defence to make you pine away the best years of your young life behind prison bars."

"I do not see that I am to be pitied," answered Albi, in the same energetic tone as before. "Every man has his ambition. That of some men is to fill a pocket with gold pieces, that of others to tie a piece of red silk round their necks; yours is, I believe, to sell more copies of your newspaper than your neighbour over the way. I have mine too, which is to establish a Republic of honest men. I care not the price I pay."

"And what is your idea of an honest man?" inquired Horace, eyeing him with curiosity.

Albi took the pipe out of his mouth and looked at him hard.

"You Gerolds are honest men," he said slowly: "your father is an honest man and a credit to human nature. Your brother promises to be like him; and I trust you will too. You have been so hitherto." And he laid a marked stress on that word *hitherto*.

CHAPTER III.

M. POCHEMOLLE'S REQUEST.

There was no more talk about the five-and-twenty thousand francs. The conspirator Albi's utterances had fallen upon the free and easy conversation like a blast of hot air, withering it up by the roots. M. de Tirecruchon lapsed silent; and, presently, two of the crop-haired inmates of the penal wing coming in to lay the luncheon-cloth, Horace Gerold and Jean Kerjou took their leave.

"Lucky dogs!" sighed the fat editor, accompanying them to the end of the passage. "Yet two months before I may taste fresh air with you." He shook Horace's hand warmly, but holding it an instant, said: "Listen, M. Gerold. You pull too strong an oar for the *Sentinelle*. You're a man of independent views, and don't like running in grooves: as well harness a race-horse to a stone-cart, as keep you on a Radical paper. Your six months will be over soon. Come to me, you will find no dogmatism, and I don't set up for lecturing my contributors as to the acquaintances they choose."

Horace coloured at this inuendo. Truth to say, he felt humiliated by the rebuke of Nestor Roche, and by the covert warning implied in the last words of Albi. Time was when he might have submitted to be sermonized by the old Republican, whom he esteemed; but success had raised his spirit, and he resented the stiffness with which the overtures of M. Macrobe, as conveyed through him, had been repulsed. There was something quite unreasonable in this frame of mind: for Nestor Roche might surely be excused for not feeling gushingly towards the man who had put him into prison; but reason is not the forte of youth; and in his pique, Horace bethought him seriously that he had a grievance against his editor.

He said as much to Jean Kerjou as they left

Sainte Pélagie; and emitted one or two bitter reflections as to the obstinacy of old Republicans.

Jean Kerjou, being a Breton, was a Legitimist and a Catholic, and one who did not understand Republicans, nor quite realize what it was they wanted. His attachment to Horace had been formed on entirely personal grounds; but as he himself wore amulets next his shirt, signed himself when he swore, and never mentioned the name of Henri V. without doffing his hat, it was a subject of wonder to him how any one of birth and talent could profess the opinions which Horace Gerold did. In a simple tone, and rather puzzled, he answered: "I can't quite make out your party; you don't seem to agree among you as we do."

"Are there no men in your party who set up for oracles?" asked Horace; the puritan sternness of Nestor Roche, and the caustic fervour of Albi, recurring to him and nettling him.

"Perhaps there may be, but I don't know them," replied the Breton, naïvely. "I am sure, though, we have none who lecture about morality as I've heard them do every time I have been in the company of Republicans. Why don't you join our paper?" he added. "Tirecruchon is a loose fish on the surface, but a good fellow underneath; and he sets us no tether, you know: our staff is like a winter soup, full of herbs of all colours; we have two or three of your hue, but we all get on together swimmingly as beans in a pot."

Similes were one of the strong points of Jean Kerjou; they garnished his eloquence as the small dice of garlic do the roast legs of mutton in the province which was his birth-place. Horace, however, made no answer; and soon they reached the Rue Ste. Geneviève, where the first person they met was the courtly M. Pochemolle, who fingered a long piece of stamped paper which he had just received from an individual with a blue bag.

"This is for you, M. Horace. Something about this morning's business, I'm afraid," he added, in a tone of condolence.

True enough. It was a summons to appear

before the Public Prosecutor, on the charge of having wilfully killed and slain one Paul Panier, commonly called de Cosaque. M. Macrobe and Jean Kerjou were both included in the summons, for having unlawfully, and of malice prepense, aided and abetted the perpetration of that crime.

Horace had already seen the Pochemolles once that morning, for on his way to Ste. Pélagie, after breakfasting with M. Macrobe, he had stopped to shake hands with Emile and show Georgette, who had been in sickly suspense since daybreak, that he was safe. He now walked into the shop with Jean Kerjou, under pretence of reading his summons, and found Georgette still pale, but with a ray of happiness in her eyes. She had just come in from out of doors, and was drawing off some tiny grey kid gloves, much smaller and finer than the daughters of drapers usually wear. So at least thought Jean Kerjou, who was observing her.

Madame Pochemolle was as gracious and smiling as it was her wont to be whenever M. Horace paid her a visit. M. Alcibiade

Pochemolle, from sheer admiration at the sight of a man who had sent a fellow-being to his last account, allowed his ell-measure to drop. According to M. Alcibiade, the next best thing to having courage enough to kill a man oneself, was to behold some one who had performed such a deed. M. Alcibiade much regretted that he himself knew not how to fence. He was not ferocious; indeed, he was rather mild than otherwise; but he thought he should like to kill some other draper's son in fair combat.

Jean Kerjou, casting his eyes about the shop, which was fitted and wainscoted with the fine old oak of a century ago, lit upon the two famous prints showing the Rue Ste. Geneviève such as it existed in the reigns of Louis XIV. and XV., and having ventured to admire these heirlooms, was soon led to discover the monarchical, aristocratical, and clerical proclivities of the Pochemolle household. The draper, his wife, and the journalist then fell into harmonious talk and regrets over those good times when kings had no legislatures to plague them, when there was a gibbet stationed permanently in front of Notre Dame, and when a tradesman of the Rue Ste. Geneviève would not so much as have eaten an egg on a Friday without leave from the Bishop of Paris. Horace followed Georgette into the little back parlour, where she went to take off her bonnet. The door remained open, but there was no reason why any words spoken there should be heard in the shop. Horace spoke low.

"You have been for a walk, Georgette?"

"No," she murmured; "it was not a walk."

"Where then?"

She looked at him with more tenderness than she was aware of in her glistening eyes:

"To church," she whispered.

"To church, Georgette! But this isn't Sunday."

"It's more than that to me," she replied, with a touching accent.

"And to what saint did you pray?"

A tear or two welled up into her eyes as she blushed and said, almost inaudibly: "Could I keep away from thanking the Virgin on the day when your life has run such dangers and been spared?"

There was so much delicate modesty in her manner of murmuring these words, and when she had uttered them the emotion that suffused her face, and the grace which love lent to her demeanour, as she wavered between the fear of having said too much and the consciousness that all she might say would ill describe the tenth of what she felt—gave her such a charm that she looked to Horace more lovely and attractive than she had ever seemed before. He gazed on her with a sort of spell-bound and astonished admiration as one contemplates a picture whose full beauties one had not at first suspected. But even as he was gazing the current of his thoughts was turned by a sudden reflection. A voice rose up within him and put the question, like a note of reproof:—Whither was all this tending, and what did he hope would be the result of the love which he was encouraging in this poor girl?

He was not flippant or profligate, and the question unsettled him. The finer feelings in his nature revolted at the thought of trifling with the affections of a woman—a child almost—who seemed to have given him her heart; and yet, except an illicit passion — seduction and its attendant ties—there was but one possible course open to him, and that was to let Georgette think that he intended marrying her; and to do so. He was not prepared for this last step; and as the conviction forced itself upon him that he was drifting into straits where no man ever yet steered right who did not arm himself with inflexible resolution, a cloud passed over his brow, and he bit his lips.

Their eyes met—hers candid and trustful, his restless and uncertain. Then he said to himself: "I must remove from this house, else there will be misfortune on us all."

He rose abruptly, shook hands with Georgette without looking at her, muttered a few words about hoping soon to see her again, and passed through the shop, telling Jean Kerjou they would meet by-and-by, but that for the present he had letters to write. He hurried upstairs to his rooms, repeating to himself in a troubled frame of mind that he must go, and would explain why to Emile when the latter came home. But before he had reached his door he heard steps behind him, and the voice of M. Pochemolle hailed him with a petition for a minute's interview : " M. Horace, sir, if you could be so kind as to give me a moment of your time. I want to ask your advice."

" Walk in," answered Horace, absently.

When they were alone together—M. Pochemolle planted on a chair, and rubbing his ear to find a suitable exordium ; Horace seated at his desk, expecting it was a legal opinion that was going to be asked of him—the draper began : " It's about Georgette, sir."

Horace started, and felt moisture bedewing his forehead.

" Yes, it's about my Georgette, sir," continued M. Pochemolle, not noticing anything. "If I might make so bold as to say so, M. Horace, I look upon you almost as an old friend now. You're a wiser man too than I am, notwithstanding your years, which comes of learning; and I want you to give me advice. To tell you the truth, sir, our Georgette has not been well of late; I told your honoured brother, M. Emile, so the other day. She's grown thin and pale, and doesn't talk as she used to do, nor laugh, nor seem to care much for things: all of which signs have been alarming her mother and me. But you know how women are, sir, and I don't think my wife and I would be likely to agree about our child's ailment, nor about the remedy for it. I ascribe a good deal of it to study and book-reading" (Horace gave a sigh of relief), "which is very well for men,—at least, for gentlemen—but isn't worth a rush for women. My respected mother—God bless her!—never read in any book save her ledger and her breviary, and this didn't prevent her making a true wife and a fine woman of business. But in these times old customs are dying out, and nothing would serve my wife but to have our Georgette brought up at a convent, where they taught her to strum on the piano, and paint flowers, and tell straight off on her fingers' ends who was Pope of Rome five hundred years ago, which seems to me about as useless knowledge for a tradesman's daughter as well can be. However, it was no good my attempting to say anything, for when I wanted our Georgette to be taught cooking, and book-keeping, and all that makes a useful housewife, her mother wouldn't hear of it. My wife, you see, is of the modern sort. She wants me to make haste and get rich, and outshine our neighbours, and be a finer man than my father was; and as for Georgette, she dresses her up in silk, and counts upon marrying her to some gentleman who'll be several cuts above us, and shut his door in our faces when we go and call upon our child. Now, that's all very well in its way, but in Georgette's own interest, M. Horace, I want to prevent it. Not that I should grudge my daughter a husband after her own fancy, if I thought she had set her heart upon any one, and I found the man was respectable and paid his bills punctually; but I don't think she has; and there's a youth I've in my mind who's in love with her, and a very thrifty, intelligent lad into the bargain, who'd be sure to make her happy, and I should like to bring the two together."

Horace took up a quill, and hacked it with a pen-knife.

"Who is this youth, M. Pochemolle?"

"Well, sir, he's a commercial traveller. He's not often in Paris, but when he does come he lodges up on the sixth floor above our heads, renting a room there all the year round. He's a cheerful young man, always ready — too ready some say—to crack his joke, and has known our Georgette ever since they were both no higher than this chair."

"Indeed!" broke in Horace, rather drily; "is it the gentleman I have met once or twice on the staircase, who wears a Scotch tartan waistcoat, with a brass chain over it, rattles pence in his pockets, and whistles the *Marseillaise* every time he comes upstairs?"

"That's he I daresay," assented M. Pochemolle thoughtfully; "though I've never heard him whistle the *Marseillaise;* but his chain's gold, M. Horace, I assure you, and probably eighteen-carat, for he's very well off. His name's Filoselle; he's been travelling since he was twenty, getting five per cent. profit on all his commissions, and he's now twenty-eight, which makes a good deal of money. If he marries our Georgette, as he hopes to do, he means to set up in business for himself with the savings he has laid by."

Horace closed his pen-knife with a snap.

"And in what way can I assist you, M. Pochemolle?" he inquired.

"Well, sir," responded the draper, too intent upon his own thoughts to remark aught unusual in the tone of his lodger,—"Well, sir, M. Filoselle is a great favourite with us all, on account of his amusing ways. I sometimes think he'd make a stuffed bird laugh would that young man. Of a winter evening, when he's in Paris, he often comes in, and makes himself sociable, telling stories, and playing tricks with cards, and the like; and turning the things upside down; and my wife thinks well of him, I'm sure; but between that and accepting him as a husband for Georgette, is a long way; and, as for Georgette herself, why, I fancy she looks upon him as an old playfellow, but nothing else: so that Filoselle feels in a fix, and last time he was here, he told me that he shouldn't like to touch upon the question with the women downstairs until I had put in a good word for him."

Here M. Pochemolle shrugged his shoulders, and continued, dolefully, "But my putting in a good word would be just about as much use as arguing with a deaf post. My wife is a good woman, and I don't say but that she and I have got on smoothly together; but there's no tackling her about her daughter. On that point she's hoighty-toity, and as foolish as women are when they get any fixed idea into their heads. I think, though, M. Horace" (and here the honest draper became appealing),—"I think you might help us. My wife has a high opinion of you, which is only natural and properly respectful on her part, and supposing, for instance, one day you had dropped into the shop by hazard like, I was to set the talk rolling on commercial travellers, and you were to join in and say there wasn't a more honourable profession going, and that they earned a deal of money, and were quite on a level with gentlemen, I think, sir, that might settle it."

M. Pochemolle fixed his eyes interrogatively on Horace.

"And have you yourself this high opinion of commercial travellers?" asked the latter.

"Well, I've a good opinion of those who get on in the business," answered the draper. "My wife she's all for scented gentlemen—even when they've got nothing in their pockets, which is less seldom than one supposes. If she could, she'd make a gentleman of me. As it is, she talked me into doing what I'd never done in my life before—invest money in one of those giant new companies that are all full like a balloon to-day and all squash like nothing to-morrow. Happily, it's the Crédit Parisien, which, M. Macrobe tells me, is as safe as the Bank of France—and there's no denying it pays up well, and the shares are rising like quicksilver; but, to speak my mind, M. Horace, I don't fancy those kind of things.

It's always been a motto in our family to sell fairly, to be content with few customers but good, and to look to small profits but safe; and the man I want for my son-in-law is a man who thinks like me as nearly as possible—as I believe Filoselle does. He's not a genius, maybe, though geniuses behind the counter seem to me as much out of place as whales in a fish-tank; but he's a shrewd fellow, who'll give his wife a good home, never let himself be caught with chaff, and keep clear of the Tribunal de Commerce."

The two purple ears, which ornamented the sides of M. Pochemolle's head like the handles of a jug, deepened in hue as he concluded the panegyric of his prospective son-in-law, and looked at the young barrister for an answer.

Had Horace prayed for it he could not have lighted upon a better opportunity of bringing his as yet innocent but dangerous *liaison* with Georgette to an end. Nevertheless (O consistency of human nature!) the idea of Georgette being married now caused him, of a sudden, unaccountable vexation bordering on jealousy. He dismissed M. Pochemolle with a vague assurance that he would see about the matter, and do his best; and, when the good man had departed, happy with having obtained his powerful co-operation, he paced about his room, pondering how he might best thwart this intended marriage. Such is man where women are concerned—a being more capricious than woman herself.

Of course he did not acknowledge to himself of what nature were the feelings that prompted him to think as he was doing, for the human mind, in its queerest fits of selfishness, is ever ingenious at putting a colour of honesty on its schemes. He argued with himself that Georgette was too good for this commercial traveller, who wore a tartan waistcoat, and looked like a snob; that he would be doing her a service in preventing her being tied for life to this man; that she was a refined, well-educated girl, who deserved a better fate, &c. &c. The Devil, who was close at hand, found him logic as much as he needed.

Whilst he was thus brooding peevishly, not very well-pleased with himself, he strayed into his brother's room, and stopped, with his eyes fixed on the portrait of his and Emile's mother hanging over the mantelpiece.

Their mother was as a dim vision to both the brothers, for she had died when they were too young to miss the guiding spirit they were losing. Horace, however, being by three years the eldest, could remember more than Emile, and he would often gaze abstractedly at the portrait, trying to recall a living image from out of the faint pencilled features. He did so now; and the effect upon him was soothing and beneficial as all thoughts of a loved and lost mother must be. Whilst he looked, the unworthy impulses within him seemed slowly to subside, then to melt. His better nature regained the mastery. He felt ashamed of having wavered even for a moment, and took the resolution there and then to do his duty. "I must not see Georgette again," he murmured; "and I had better do what her father wishes—put in a word for this tradesman."

"Ah! they told me you were at home," cried

a voice behind him. "I've come to fetch you off to dinner. You know we've got things to talk about. We're going to be tried for manslaughter together."

And M. Macrobe, who had intruded himself noiselessly into the room, held out his hand.

Horace gave a start, but he shook the hand, though it seemed to him that in doing so he was swearing friendship to a sort of black-coated Mephistopheles.

CHAPTER IV.

M. MACROBE INSERTS THE THIN END OF THE WEDGE.

M. MACROBE's face was against him, but if you gave him half-an-hour to talk it away, and another half-hour to make you forget the suspicious stories you had heard concerning him, he was a pleasant companion. He took Horace to dine at his own house in the Avenue des Champs Elysées: not a formal repast with guests eyeing one another ceremoniously over white neck-ties, but what he called a quiet dinner *sans façon*, to which he had invited a few nice fellows, and at which there were no ladies present. Our young friend was a little surprised at the luxury of the banker's residence, to which he had as yet seen nothing comparable, not even in the one or two lordly mansions of the

Faubourg St. Germain where it had been his fate to visit. Everything, from the glossy livery of the porter, who swung open the gilt bronze gates as they drove up, down to the cypher and crest engraved on the massive plate of the dinner-table, bore the impress of solid, although new-made wealth. It was not foolish wealth however, such as does not know where to bestow itself, and heaps around it vulgar and cumbersome splendour which dazzles without exciting admiration. M. Macrobe had seen too much of life not to have learned good taste. As he ushered his guest through a series of spacious and elegantly appointed saloons into a dining-room teeming with brilliancy and light, he flattered himself that if there were houses in Paris equal to his own, there were few superior, and he was not wrong.

The emotions of the day had been so numerous and varied that they had slightly unnerved Horace, and disposed him to accept any diversion as welcome. He was in that state of mind when friendliness comes as a balm, and slight attentions are received with a gratitude deeper sometimes than the occasion warrants. His duel of the morning—the gloomy horror of which was beginning to strike him with dull force now that he was cool and could reason;—his unsatisfactory interview with Nestor Roche; the doubts that he could not altogether allay as to the conduct he ought to have adopted and should adopt in the future towards Georgette; all these were harassing topics, which he was glad to dismiss for a while from his agitated brain. So the dinner was a relief to him, and, therefore, from M. Macrobe's point of view, a success. That gentleman had indeed spared nothing to make it so. The viands were choice, the conversation agreeable, and the guests all men famous in their respective walks, who treated Horace with a courteous deference that flattered him. Jean Kerjou was there, endowed with the excellent appetite that befitted his mediæval tastes, and, like his friend, not sorry to place the fumes of champagne between himself and the bloody scene of the morning. The Breton journalist had a constitutional horror of bloodshed—which was the more remarkable as he himself had been out twice, and each time killed his man. But, perhaps, in his opinion this did not count, for he was a fiery Papist, and the two brother-journalists he had slain were only Voltairians.

The other guests were: Baron Margauld the banker, husband to the Madame de Margauld Horace had already met in society—a grave, emphatic man, suspected of Orleanism, but respected by the Government on account of his solid credit and his unaffected detestation of Radicals; M. Arsène Gousset, a sparkling novelist, in great favour at court, and mightily popular with women, though he passed his time in railing bitterly at the former and inditing cutting satires upon the latter; and the Prince of Arcola, descended from one of the first Napoleon's Field-Marshals—a young gentleman of eight-and-twenty, with a very grand air and high tone, tempered, however, with a good-humoured listlessness, which generally rose to the surface once the ice of formalism was broken. This, with the eminent surgeon who had attended the combat in the morning, made seven who sat down to table. But presently, when the soup had been removed, and two giants were handing round turbot and salmon-trout, entered, like a rush of wind, Mr. Drydust the celebrated correspondent of a London penny paper, who, with florid grace, excused himself for being late, on the ground that he had just been having an interview with the Minister of State. It was the peculiarity and good fortune of Mr. Drydust that he was always having interviews with Cabinet Ministers.

As the duel had created a considerable sensation and was for the nonce the one subject of gossip about town, it was unavoidable that some allusion should be made to it, and that Horace should receive the congratulations which are customary under such circumstances. Mr. Drydust, especially, seemed to know more about the occurrence than the parties themselves. He had written a full-length and erroneous account of it to his paper that afternoon, and on learning that he actually had opposite to him the man who had rid Paris of the dreaded M. de Cosaque, he proceeded, somewhat to the dismay of M. Macrobe, to rattle off with immense volubility, and in first-rate French, the names of all the illustrious persons of his acquaintance who had fought duels—winding up with the case of two distinguished British nobles who had wished to exterminate one another on Calais sands, but had been happily prevented by his timely interference. Horace listened with a rather embarrassed air; and Jean Kerjou furtively made the sign of the cross, in obedience to the superstition which holds it unlucky to speak of slaughter at table. But Mr. Drydust soon turned his attention to other themes. He apostrophized the Prince of Arcola:

"Prince, I was at Chantilly the day before yesterday, and saw your filly, *Mogador*, do her canter. Take my advice and back her in preference to her stable-companion, *Namouna*, for the *Prix de Diane*. I was talking about it to Lagrange; he thinks she'll win."

"Ah!" said the Prince, languidly, "I thought Count de Lagrange had got a filly of his own in the race."

"So he has; but I told him it wasn't worth a stiver. Lord Martingale was of the same opinion."

"Why, what has come over the filly then? Last week Lord Martingale backed her against my stable at five to one."

The Prince of Arcola had two passions: horse-racing and nobility. On the first he spent two-thirds of his income, which was large; on the second he lavished what spare time he had, reading books of heraldry and chivalrous chronicles. It was a most sore point with him that his title dated no further back than half a century, and had been conferred, in a batch, by a Napoleon. He would have bartered it with all his heart, high-sounding as it was, for a simple barony of mediæval creation; and when M. Macrobe whispered to him, in introducing Horace Gerold, that this was the young barrister who might call himself Marquis of Clairefontaine if he chose, he eyed Horace much as one contemplates a phenomenon, and soon set the conversation going on the Castle of Hautbourg, which he appeared to know from roof to basement, furniture included, as if he had been residing there for the last twelvemonth. He had a way of talking, when launched on his favourite topics, which lacked neither fire nor grace; and Horace followed him with a secret and altogether new interest as he dilated with enthusiasm on the broad acres, grey towers, old pictures, arms and sculptured halls of Hautbourg. "One of the finest domains I know," said he, "in this or any other country. Do you often go down there for shooting?" he added: and this question breaking the spell, Horace answered, a little drily, that he never went there at all. Whereat the Prince stared, and by-and-by observed with a sigh: "Political conviction must be very strong, M. Gerold, to make one renounce such treasures. *I* couldn't do it."

Mr. Drydust, who was patronizing the banker Margauld, giving him information as to scrip and share, current quotations, and the prospects of the new Irrawaddi loan, here cut in. He had caught the word "shooting," and immediately started upon a description of the great estates with which he was familiar—Windsor Castle, Knowsley,

Chatsworth, Stowe, Eaton Court, &c.: all places where, by his own account, he was wont to go and divert himself with a few weeks' sport when he had nothing better to do. His rapid sketches were so vivid and well-coloured that M. Arsène Gousset, deferring modestly to him as a superior genius, remarked how much democratic France was behind aristocratic England from the artist's point of view.

"With our code of equality and our parcelling of land," said he, "we have suppressed great wealth and pomp, and, consequently, picturesqueness. Wishing to be all of a size, we have dragged the nobles off their high towers and forced them to stand shoulder to shoulder with us in a flat plain, where no man's head may rise above those of his fellows under pain of making the rest cry out. French society has become a landscape without hills, a sea without waves, a house without gables;—anything you please that is dull and commonplace. It may be correct, but it is very ugly."

"Yet equality is one of the first conditions of

progress," remarked the eminent surgeon; who, like most eminent surgeons, professed extreme liberalism, the more so at this moment, as he had expected to be made surgeon to the court, but been disappointed.

"Ah! progress," exclaimed the novelist, with a shrug, as he put down a glass of Tokay,—"progress, doctor, is a word coined by journalists and barristers, to signify that now-a-days it is they who rule the roast. We have superseded the nobles, and given ourselves for a prey to the men who talk and the men who write, and we call that abolishing caste rule. They say merit has better chances than it used to have; but, pray, when was merit more respected than when low-born Froissart consorted on terms of equality with the proudest noblemen of France? when Rabelais, a witty curate, was the friend of Francis the First? when Charles the Ninth did homage in verse to Ronsard? and when Louis the Fourteenth himself, who would not have bared his head to an emperor, waited at table upon Molière? If we look past history through, we shall scarce find a man of any worth in art, politics, or science, who was not petted, honoured, and enriched by the great of his time. With all our boast of progress and equality, there is not a court in Europe that would receive a goldsmith as Benvenuto Cellini was received at the Court of France; there is not a potter of our day who could hope to win the distinctions that Bernard de Palissy earned. Charles the Fifth of France ennobled the man who set up the first clock; did we do as much for the man who invented photography? Gutemberg, it is true, led a struggling life, but was George Stephenson's path strewn with roses? and of the two, which, think you, were most to blame, the mediævals who were tardy to acknowledge the advantages of writing by machinery instead of by hand, or the moderns who, after recognizing what they term the benefits of railways, suffered the inventor to be laid in the earth without a single token of gratitude from the state? In politics, again, because we stock our cabinets with superannuated lawyers and jaded leader-writers, carefully excluding the rest of the world, we cry out that we have thrown open a broad career to talent, just as if our ancestors had not done so before us, and more liberally. What were Richelieu and Colbert but friendless men of middle-class estate, who, by mere dint of adroitness, acquired the patronage of powerful noblemen, by whom they were introduced and pushed forward at court? The fact is, any man with brains and pleasant manners could make his way in former times, and was not obliged to wait until his teeth were loose and his hair fell off, as seems to be indispensable in our day. A fellow of parts attached himself to the suite of a noble, became his patron's adviser, then his friend, was presented to the king, flattered him — and why not? I would as lief flatter a king to obtain a bunch of seals as a ragamuffin to catch a vote — and with a little patience and wit rose to be Prime Minister, like the two I have named; or High Chancellor, like L'Hôpital and Harlay; or Marshal of France, like Turenne and Catinat (who were the sons of small country gentlemen); or Bishop, like Bossuet and Fléchier, — the latter of whom was bred a tallow-chandler.

The best of it was, too, that we took these men young, when their intellects were in their vigour: for progress had not yet made it a law that our statesmen should be old men stricken with the gout, and our generals aged cripples, with all the genius frozen out of them by rheumatism. Had they lived in our day, Richelieu would have been, at thirty, a curate with fifty napoleons a year; Turenne a lieutenant, wondering whether he should ever be a major; and Colbert a government clerk in the office of Mr. Drydust's friend, Monsieur Gribaud."

Mr. Drydust nodded assent. He thought the atmosphere of modern civilization stifling. Nevertheless, he was in favour of penny papers. All things considered, he should like to be living under Louis XI., with the cheap press flourishing as an institution.

But the novelist was averse to such a combination. He was not fond of the Press, and took no pains to conceal it. Cracking filberts composedly, and smiling within his well-trimmed yellow beard, he amused himself and the rest of the table by passing in review the Paris Press, and grimly bespattering the whole journalistic profession, without bitterness, but without mercy. He made an exception in favour of the *Sentinelle* and the *Gazette des Boulevards*, out of respect for the two writers present; but he could not refrain from giving a side cuff to the editors of those journals, MM. de Tirecruchon and Roche: the former of whom he described as the most agreeable humbug he knew, and the latter as a vinegar-cruet—cold without and sour within. It was pleasure to watch the starched features of the Baron Margauld relax whilst this performance was going on. He, too, was no friend of the Press: " a dangerous, meddlesome institution," as he termed it.

His satisfaction bordered upon mirth when the novelist continued: " You are right to call the Press a power, for it is a power for destruction, like gunpowder or corrosive acid: but it has never built up anything, and never will. Since daily newspapers have come among us, the word 'stability' has ceased to have any sense, and should disappear from the dictionary. Nothing is stable now-a-days: neither thrones, nor constitutions, nor religions. A journalist is a man who devotes his time to finding out the weak points in human institutions, political or social, and hammering upon them continually until the whole structure falls to pieces. There is very little discrimination in his work: for with him it is not a question of being right or wrong, but of filling up three or six columns a week. If the times be fertile in large abuses, so much the wider his choice of subjects; but if the Government be an honest one, and there be only small abuses, he will assail these small abuses at just the same length, and with precisely the same vigour of invective, as the larger ones. Louis Philippe was attacked more severely than Charles X., and the Republic of '48 more pitilessly than Louis Philippe. There is not a government on earth can bear up against the three-column system; heaven itself couldn't stand it. If ever the millennium arrives, it will have to begin by gagging the Press, else in twenty years it will go the way of all other governments."

The banker Margauld bent his head and

coughed, in token of enthusiastic concurrence. But the Prince of Arcola whispered, with a smile, to his neighbour: "I fancy M. Gousset is himself a victim of the three-column system. His last novel met with some rather rough handling, did it not?"

It was now time for coffee; and M. Macrobe rose to lead the way to his smoking-room—an apartment of sybaritish comfort and luxury, fitted up like an Arab tent, with Turkey carpets a foot thick, and low divans, into which the human form sank, stretched enjoyably at full length.

In the passage to this *buen-retiro* Mr. Drydust naturally contrived to push to the front once more as leader of the conversation,—the only post his coruscating genius brooked. Cigars, with curiously outlandish names, but of exquisite smell and savour, were produced from cedar-wood cases; the powdered gentlemen poured fragrant coffee, steaming hot, into cups small and transparent as eggshells; and whilst the fumes of Mocha, blending with those of Havannah, were rising spirally towards the ceiling, the British journalist resumed his observations upon men and things, and the company were soon wrapped in the pyrotechnic blaze of that gentleman's utterances, which were always entertaining, sometimes even dazzling to his audience. The performance was not so engrossing, however, but that the Prince of Arcola, who was seated on the same ottoman as Horace, found occasion to strike up with the latter what the French call an exchange of good proceedings. He admired the modest young barrister. He paid him compliments with that insinuating and polished grace of which the French are such masters, asked him to breakfast at his house in the Rue Lafite—one of the largest and most hospitable in the Chausseé d'Antin—and ended by offering to propose him for election at the club of the Rue Royale.

"You should belong to a club," said he: "clubs are social ménageries; one meets all the lions there. They are one of the many good things we have borrowed from the English, to whom we are indebted for pretty nearly everything that makes existence tolerable."

"I shall be happy to second you," added Baron Margauld, whom Horace struck as a quiet, earnest young man, and worth weaning from Radicalism.

Horace thanked them, but declined: for a Paris club and a London one are not quite the same things. In four cases out of five the former is little more than a sumptuous gambling-house in disguise; and of all the gambling-houses of the capital, the Cercle de la Rue Royale was the most celebrated as well as the most splendid. The Prince did not press his offer, but wondered a little that Horace should allege want of means as one of the reasons for declining it.

The court novelist volunteered on his side to introduce Gerold to some of the leading authors, and this proposal was accepted gratefully.

"I know most of the journalists," said Horace, "and I have seen Monsieur Hugo at Brussels; but I should feel it an honour to be acquainted with our other national glories—M. de Musset, M. Ponsard, M. Gautier, and Mdme. Sand." He added something gracious as a hint that he had perused all M. Arsène Gousset's works, and ranked him, too, amongst the national glories. The novelist was sensible to the homage, and, towards midnight, when Horace had retired with his friend, Jean Kerjou, after accepting the Prince of Arcola's invitation to breakfast, and making a luncheon appointment with M. Macrobe for the next day, that they might appear before the Public Prosecutor together, he exclaimed with some admiration: "Good blood will out. That young Gerold has the manners of a duke: he is serious, dignified, and absolutely unaffected. It is incomprehensible to me that he should elect to be a *sansculotte.*"

"He has fallen into bad hands," sighed M. Macrobe unctuously.

"Yes, but what makes him talk about the mediocrity of his means?" interposed the Prince of Arcola, with curiosity. "The Hautbourg estates are worth a million francs a year, if they are worth a centime. What do the Gerolds do with all their money?"

"Ah, there you put a question I should like

to solve myself," replied M. Macrobe. "The Gerolds are millionaires, I know, but they live as if they were poor. The father has a small lodging on a fifth floor at Brussels; I had inquiries made there by our correspondent. The police think they spend their fortune on secret societies; but this is probably a guess."

"There would be no derogation in it," said the Prince. "If a man of birth goes in for people's rights he is quite right to do it grandly; and there would be something not unbecoming in young Gerold putting himself at the head of an occult social movement destined to revolutionize the country. After all, he would only be re-enacting the part the Montmorencys and the Colignys played when they took the lead of the Huguenots, who were the Radicals of their time."

"For myself," chimed in the court novelist, composedly, "I should not be sorry if there were a good sanguinary break-out, like the Reign of Terror, only worse. I am convinced that if the Radicals were allowed their head for a few years, they would lead France such a gallop that she would leap madly back into royalty, feudalism, and rabid popery to get rid of them. Then we should have a century or so of peace."

"God bless my soul! you are surely not speaking in earnest," cried out the banker Margauld in disgust. He had seen revolutions face to face, and thought them no themes for jocularity. Happily Mr. Drydust was by to reassure him. According to this eminent person the Second Empire was unshakable, having the sympathies of democratic England with it. These sympathies found expression in the penny sheet, to which Mr. Drydust contributed, and were enough to keep any throne stable to all eternity. "Besides," added he, "you may make your mind perfectly easy, Baron, and you too, M. Macrobe, for M. Gerold does not spend his money on secret societies. I will tell the Prefect of Police so next time I talk to him. I know the man who is the soul of all the French secret societies: it's that arch-revolutionist Albi: he's in prison now—an intimate friend of mine—but a dark-minded character, who would no more agree with young Gerold, nor roost in the same nest with him, than a crow would with a starling." Then Mr. Drydust proceeded to explain how secret societies were organized; after which he speculated as to how the Gerolds spent their money; but eventually finding the problem insoluble, branched off into a disquisition upon "odd people," whose lives were a mystery to the community. M. Macrobe reiterated his regrets that Gerold had fallen into bad hands, and Mr. Drydust assented. He further engaged to bring him back by degrees to the right way, by giving him as much of his society as was compatible with his— Mr. Drydust's—other and multifarious occupations.

Meanwhile, the subject of these remarks, rolling homewards in a cab, was reflecting with satisfaction on the delicate, and even generous, behaviour of M. Macrobe: for just as Horace was leaving, the financier had drawn him aside and said: "My dear young friend, I am not surprised at M. Roche having refused the twenty-five thousand francs: for, though honest, I fancy he is a little opiniated—isn't he?—and not quite exempt from narrow-mindedness. Such at least is the character he has always borne in the Press, and, if you will allow me to say so, I have heard it deplored that a man of your wonderful and shining abilities should be tied to the same wheel as a person so cramped in intellect. The money must now go to the poor, and here I should really esteem it a favour if you could recommend me any worthy persons on whom to bestow it. As a liberal writer, you are, probably, often besieged with applications from needy people, whose political opinions make it difficult for them to obtain relief through the usual channels. There must be numerous families of poor Republicans who took part in the affair of '48, and who would stand no chance of obtaining anything from the Municipal Bureaux de Bienfaisance: these are the very people I should like to assist. And now, as to this trial of ours, I suppose you are aware that, from a certain point of view, it is a less serious matter to kill one's adversary in a duel than to wound him. If you wound him, you are tried in the Correctional Court by three judges, without jury, and you are safe to be imprisoned; in the other case, you are arraigned at the Assizes before a jury, and are invariably acquitted. However, we shall have to prepare a defence of some sort, and so I have been thinking we could not do better than have one counsel for the three of us, and that counsel your own brother, whose abilities I hear so warmly eulogized. The trial will be sure to draw a great crowd, and will help him forward in his profession. I shall instruct my solicitor to offer him my brief, and I trust you will prevail upon him to accept it."

"It was thoughtful," mused Horace; "and it was gracious. The man is a gentleman, and it is a pity I ever joined in calumniating him."

CHAPTER V.

HOW EMPIRES ARE GOVERNED.

On the morrow, at about the time when Horace Gerold, Jean Kerjou, and M. Macrobe were being minutely cross-questioned by the Public Prosecutor as to their motives for maliciously slaying an official journalist, his Excellency M. Gribaud, Minister of State, was holding audiences at his residence in the Louvre, and it was noticed by all whom applications for patronage, favours, or redress brought into contact with that great man, that his Excellency was not at all in a good humour that morning.

Towards mid-day M. Camille de Beaufeuillet, one of the Minister's secretaries, a grave diplomatic young gentleman of irreproachable attire, issued from his chief's presence, and remarked to a brother secretary in an ante-room: "The governor has turned out of bed the wrong side this morning."

"Ah!" exclaimed the other, with an intonation that betokened neither amazement nor great concern; and looking up from the *Moniteur* with which he was beguiling the tedium of business hours, he added: "Summer heat doesn't agree with the old fellow; he's been bitter as a weed this some time past."

"He has sent me out to take stock of the unfortunates who are kicking their heels about in the waiting-rooms," resumed M. de Beaufeuillet; and saying this, he touched a bell on the table.

An usher with a silver chain round his neck, appeared.

"Is the slate very full, Bernard?"

"Very, sir; I much fear his Excellency will have a heavy morning; there are above twenty people waiting." And at the bidding of the young man, the venerable Bernard recapitulated the names of all the persons in attendance—a goodly list, on which figured many ladies of beauty come to solicit distinctions for their husbands; many gentlemen devoid of beauty, but replete with ambition, come to beg honours for themselves; and a remanet of individuals whose errands were purely disinterested and undertaken only from a desire to serve the State. Amongst these last was our friend Mr. Drydust, who stated that his business was important.

"I think you had better show in the English journalist first," hazarded M. Camille. "I believe the Government considers him useful."

But at that moment, entered a second usher, who said: "M. Louchard, the Commissary of Police, has just arrived." An intimation which caused the secretary to vanish for a minute, and, on returning, to say: "M. Louchard takes precedence of everybody. His Excellency will see him at once."

In another couple of minutes M. Louchard, the commissary, had been conducted deferentially through the ante-room, and was closeted in private with the Minister. The two secretaries pulled

faces behind him when he had passed; but this
M. Louchard did not notice.

His Excellency M. Gribaud was one of the
bulwarks of the Second Empire. Formerly, he
had been one of the bulwarks of the Republic, and
indeed it was his mission, in a general way, to
be the bulwark of every party that happened
to be in the ascendant. In appearance, he
somewhat belied his Christian name of Augustus,
for he was not august at all; but he had a
curious penetrating eye, that partook of the
vulture's and the money-lender's, and a tongue
as pointed and insinuating as a gimlet. It was
this tongue that had helped to make the fortune
of M. Gribaud. Most people when speaking in
public are apt to hesitate now and then to find
the correct term: but not so M. Gribaud.
Nobody had ever known him pause for a word.
Correct or no, he spoke straight on with imperturbable assurance, and the policy he pursued in
elocution he followed, also, in all the aims of
his life—never allowing himself to be impeded by
a scruple, nor baulked by a regard for others.

Such a man was sure to succeed. He was just the Minister to ride rough-shod over opposition, for there was no silencing him, and he was not in the least particular as to his choice of argumentative weapons. If pressed close by the logic of an adversary, he quietly called him a liar. One of his greatest oratorical triumphs had been obtained by accusing an honourable political opponent of being sold to a foreign government. He had no proofs to support the charge, but neither had his antagonist any to refute it; and, in such cases, it is always the more worthy of the contending parties — *i.e.* the man in office—who is believed. The charge almost broke the heart of the political opponent, but it greatly added to the credit of M. Gribaud, who came to be looked upon in Imperialist circles as a debater of no ordinary value.

When the Commissary of Police entered, M. Gribaud was seated at his desk, dressed in black clothes too large for him, and a stiff white cravat, that gave him the appearance of an unusually ferocious Dissenting minister. With a thick, knotty hand he was holding up a pair of double eyeglasses, through which he scrutinized, narrowly and frowningly, a despatch from a prefect. At sight of M. Louchard he wasted no time in vain courtesies, but cried out, "I can't make out what your agents are about, M. Louchard. They never tell one anything. All the information I get as to passing events comes from private sources. Two Roman republicans spent the day before yesterday in Paris, and you were quite ignorant of the fact; yet your orders are to keep the closest watch upon every Italian who sets foot in the city."

"I am sure they did not put up at any hotel, your Excellency," pleaded M. Louchard, humbly but firmly, "else I should have known it, and sent you a report."

"They came by the mail-train from England, and returned the same night. Your detectives at the railway-terminus should have recognized them for Italians, and followed them. Had they been bent upon assassinating any of us, they might have done it with complete security. But that is not all. Why have I had no report about the three medical students, who hissed a loyal song at a music-hall last Monday night? nor about M. Giroux-Ette, my predecessor in office, and a senator, who, on Tuesday, conversed amicably for a whole hour in a public place with the Radical barrister, Claude Febvre? nor about Madame de Masseline, the wife of an official deputy, who spoke slightingly of me at one of her dinner-parties?—Why have I been apprised of none of these circumstances? The police are growing either blind or careless, M. Louchard."

"Not blind or careless, your Excellency," protested M. Louchard, with meekness; "but the police have a great deal to do, and it is difficult for them to be everywhere at once."

"What is the use of them, then?" retorted the Minister, roughly. "It is the business of the police to have their eyes everywhere. We don't stint you with money. You should see into every house as if its walls were of glass."

"We do our best," muttered M. Louchard.

"There are few houses of consequence where we have not one or two emissaries on the visiting list. Madame de Masseline herself is most zealous in conveying information as to all she hears, and I am certain that if she allowed herself to speak disparagingly of your Excellency, it was rather for the purpose of sounding her guests than to emit any opinion of her own."

"Humph!" murmured his Excellency, who appeared less certain than the police official. "I did not know Madame de Masseline was on your books, M. Louchard. If I were you I would rely as little as possible on women; their information is seldom accurate, and there is generally some woman's quarrel or jealous pique at the bottom of their denunciations. I have noticed they never tell tales of a man who has a good figure and curly hair, unless they have been jilted by him. But enough of this. What have you got to tell me this morning?"

"I have come about this Gerold affair—this duel," began M. Louchard. "I thought your Excellency might have some orders to give me."

"A pretty piece of work that duel," grumbled the Minister, his brow darkening. "You suffered this pestilent young Radical to kill one of our most serviceable writers; yet you had several hours' notice of the duel, and might easily have stopped it."

"I counted that matters would turn out differently. I imagined M. de Cosaque would kill M. Gerold," observed the commissary, naïvely.

"You don't seem very lucky in your calculations," was the Minister's dry answer; but he passed lightly over the subject, for he too had known of the duel beforehand, and if he had not thought expedient to stop it, there is a presumption that some such motive lay uppermost in his mind as had actuated M. Louchard. He remained silent a moment, stroking his short pointed chin with his hard hand, and peering with a brooding expression at the commissary. Perhaps during that moment he recalled the time when the two young Gerolds were bright boys, whom he used to go and see at school, and when their father was a friend whom he honoured and by whom he was esteemed. Those were far-off days, and probably the remembrance of them was not over-pleasant: for M. Gribaud broke out morosely: "Look here, M. Louchard: I've had enough of this M. Horace Gerold. Things were going on very well before he turned up; the Opposition were almost silent: but now it looks as if the old nonsense were coming back. This young Gerold is becoming a power. People talk about him in society, he has all the women on his side; in a word, he is dangerous. It is time you saw to him. That was a very suspicious document you showed me some time ago—I mean that deed of gift. If those two youths are already possessors of the Hautbourg estate, they are millionaires, and their leading the bread-and-water life they do is a queer circumstance that has a strong smell of conspiracy about it. You must have a close surveillance set upon both the brothers; they must not be lost sight of a minute; you must ascertain what they do, where they go, whom they see: their letters must be opened at the post-office, and if you discover that they habitually frequent or correspond with men of extreme opinions, there will be enough in that to furnish a handle to the Public Prosecutor. At all events — and I hope you understand me, M. Louchard — M. Horace Gerold must be got rid of; we must frighten him into running back to Belgium, and if he won't go, why" (M. Gribaud threw a significant glance at the commissary)— "why I daresay it won't be very difficult to send him where tougher men than he have gone—on a forced voyage to Cayenne."

Accustomed as M. Louchard was to the mention of Cayenne and Lambessa as fitting places of resort for Liberals, and animated as he moreover was, against Horace Gerold by the recollection of how the latter had treated him on the occasion of the domiciliary visit, he felt a creeping sensation in the back at the grim coolness of the Minister's tone. M. Gribaud, indeed, made no more bones about removing an enemy from his path than about filliping a speck of dust off his coat. The commissary answered with his usual abject deference:

"It shall be done as your Excellency wishes." Then he twirled his hat for a few moments between his fingers, as if doubtful whether to proceed with certain other communications he had intended making, until, finally, a thought seemed to strike him, and he said:—" If your Excellency will allow me to express an opinion, I think M. Horace Gerold, though dangerous, may turn out to be less so than his brother. My men have had their eyes on both for some time, and M. Emile is the one who appears to me the most vicious. He never goes into society nor to the theatre; he works very hard; he has few friends, and those all of the worst sort—hardened Republicans; he distributes a great deal of money amongst the poor, and visits them at their own houses; he also lends them books, which I take to be a mischievous symptom: for the poor who read become unmanageable. M. Horace, I am bound to say, is just the contrary. He mixes a good deal with everybody, and just now he has got into good hands—those of M. Macrobe, the banker, your Excellency. If your Excellency would have very precise information as to M. Horace Gerold's sayings and doings, there is not a better man to apply to than M. Macrobe. He had M. Gerold to dinner with him last night; and being a most loyal Imperialist, deeply attached to your Excellency, I can vouch that he would completely enter into your views with regard to watching the young man and reporting all he saw."

A belief in M. Macrobe—that is, in the man whose financial science was so profound, and whose hints were such a godsend to those on whom he deigned to bestow them—was one of the articles of M. Louchard's creed. He therefore turned completely sallow when in a short tone M. Gribaud replied :—" M. Macrobe is coming here presently, and possibly I may have to give you some instructions concerning *him*, M. Louchard. I have sent for him to explain his conduct in overtly taking part against a Government writer in a public restaurant, and in assisting this M. Gerold as second. M. Macrobe is a gentleman who had best mind his *p*'s and *q*'s. He has been tolerated because he was useful; but if he thinks himself strong enough to indulge in vagaries, he must be shown he is mistaken."

M. Louchard dug his right hand deep into one of the hind pockets of his coat, and drew from it a yellow bandanna handkerchief, of which he proceeded to make a sudden and noisy use. Had any of the familiars of the commissary been present, they would have recognized in this behaviour the infallible portent of extreme bewilderment, such as could only have arisen from the violence of internal emotion. M. Louchard, indeed, would as soon have expected to hear M. Gribaud attack his Majesty the Emperor as the powerful Director of the Crédit Parisien. M. Gribaud, who could not be supposed to know this, added sharply: "Have you anything further to say, M. Louchard; time is scarce and I've none to waste?"

"I—I—had one or two other observations to suggest," stammered M. Louchard, making an effort to rally; "but another occasion will do— when your Excellency is less engaged."

"I am not likely to be less engaged until I am out of office," rejoined the Minister with dryness.

"If you have anything to say, out with it at once."

Just then there was a knock, and the venerable Bernard glided into the room. He whispered a few words to the statesman, and withdrew.

"Here is M. Macrobe just come," remarked the latter, addressing M. Louchard. "So make haste, please."

Perhaps it was the timely reflection that after all, M. Macrobe was very well able to take care of himself, and would, in all probability, not fail to do so when necessary, or perhaps it was simply the long-acquired habit of never letting himself be long troubled by a care about others, that caused M. Louchard abruptly to shake off his momentary stupefaction, and to discharge in a business-like manner the remainder of the errand on which he had come.

"I desire to recommend to your Excellency's indulgence, a journalist at present undergoing imprisonment," said he. "It is M. de Tirecruchon, the editor of the *Gazette des Boulevards*."

"I know him well," responded his Excellency:

"as troublesome a scribbler as any in France. His paper is always turning me into ridicule."

"He is certainly troublesome," assented M. Louchard. "But he often rendered us small services, and would do more if coaxed and humoured a little. He is not a penman who could be bought with cash, like several other of the Opposition writers in our pay; but small favours would go a long way with him; they would be a profitable investment."

"Humph!" grumbled his Excellency.

"Besides," insinuated the commissary, "he has already been in prison some time, and we should only be remitting two months of his sentence. Your Excellency knows the *Gazette des Boulevards* is a paper with which it is politic, so far as is possible, to keep on good terms. Everybody reads it, and, though professing to be independent, it gives us valuable assistance in discrediting the Republicans, whom it jeers at, and unmasks most praiseworthily. Since its editor has been in prison, however, it has been dead against us, and most biting in its sarcasms. I think if we were to free M. de Tirecruchon, and offer him some small facilities in the way of sale, such as allowing his paper to be sent into the provinces by the parcels'-delivery, which would give him a start of the other journals, who are obliged to send theirs by post, we should find ourselves the better for it."

"Well, well, I'll see," growled the great M. Gribaud. "I don't like your M. de Tirecruchon. He's one of your confounded, sneering Parisians who respect nothing and nobody. I don't see that he can be better than where he is, and I wish we had all the other journalists in Paris under the same lock with him, and could keep them there to all eternity—that I do. But I'll tell you what, M. Louchard: If we release this man and throw him a bone, it must be an understood thing that his paper leaves off poking fun at me. It may laugh at my colleagues if it pleases—it's not my business to defend them—but it must respect me—and—and the Emperor," added M. Gribaud, after a moment's pause. "Do you understand, M. Louchard? If it doesn't, mind you, I'll make it unpleasant for M. de Tirecruchon. —Is that all you've got to say?"

"I wished to speak to your Excellency about Monsieur Drydust," rejoined the commissary.

"Ah! Monsieur Drydust," echoed the Minister, whose countenance at once changed and lost its stiffness. "We must be civil to him, M. Louchard. He is an ally. He writes in a paper read by a hundred thousand English shopkeepers, who'll believe what he tells them, as if it were in the Bible. We send him invitations to all the ministerial parties, and he inserts everything we ask him. Such a man must be encouraged. If he makes any request of you, that is, within the bounds of feasibility, you must accede to it."

"He often comes to the Prefecture for information," answered M. Louchard; "and so I've been thinking we could serve him and ourselves at the same time, by furnishing him with a daily bulletin, summarizing all the intelligence the Government might desire to see propagated. We would have this bulletin drawn up in English by one of our British employés, who would add such comments as we dictated to him. Gradually, Monsieur Drydust would find it the shortest way to forward our bulletin, purely and simply, to his paper: so that it will be like having a daily column in that journal at our disposal. One can insert a great deal in a column," added M. Louchard, by way of parenthesis.

M. Gribaud never fell into the bad habit of praising his subalterns, but, with a keen glance, he nodded approval.

"That reminds me I've Monsieur Drydust waiting in an ante-room all this while," said he. "Look in upon him as you go out, M. Louchard. Tell him that you will have a packet of special information ready for him every day. Mind you say *special information*. And, stay, I am so busy this morning I am really afraid I shan't have time to talk to him. Put him off politely — very politely; and give him some bit of confidential news. What shall it be? . . . Ay, this will do — and it's a good idea: Hint to him that you are on the scent of a conspiracy against the Emperor's life: mention it mysteriously, and he will be sure to make it public. Designate the chiefs of the Republican party as implicated; hint clearly at M. Horace Gerold, though don't specify him by name. Monsieur Drydust's imagination will do the rest, and his remarks will prepare the public mind, should we decide upon arresting and indicting these two Gerolds. Do that adroitly, M. Louchard; and now, good morning."

The commissary made a respectful obeisance, his eyes quavering half with admiration, half with awe at the subtle spirit of the politician facing him. Then, his business being over, he departed.

It was now the turn of the other postulants. A few days before, on learning that M. Macrobe, of the Crédit Parisien, was in attendance, M. Gribaud would have had him introduced without a moment's delay. M. Macrobe was in favour then; but the part taken by him in the duel had entirely reversed the good dispositions of M. Gribaud—who, to mark his displeasure, resolved to let the financier wait until the whole list of visitors was exhausted — that is, possibly two hours. And no doubt he would have done so but for a circumstance altogether without precedent in ante-chamber annals: for scarcely had M. Louchard retired, than the venerable Bernard entered, and, with the look of a man hopelessly flustered by the audacity of the message he is commissioned to deliver, said : " Your Excellency, M. Macrobe has desired me to say that, having numerous calls on his time this day, he would be thankful if your Excellency could either see him immediately, or grant him an audience for some appointed hour on another day."

The venerable Bernard stood still, expecting, but prepared for a thunderclap.

The great M. Gribaud answered calmly: " Show him in."

M. Macrobe was ushered in. He was attired in the black kid-gloves which constituted his gala costume ; his brass-clasped note-book was peeping out of his breast-pocket ; and at his button-hole glared, scarlet as a poppy, the ribbon of his Order. He was collected and impenetrable.

With perfect composure he made his bow, and,

in a tone that struck surprise into the Minister, from its firmness, said : "Your Excellency must excuse me : my hours are not my own, but my shareholders'. Time was when I could have afforded to wait two hours in an ante-room, but this is so no longer."

There was something very significant in this phrase. Thought the Minister to himself: "If this man is so impertinent, it is that he feels himself strong, and has allies with him more powerful than myself. Don't let us commit any blunder." And, like a prudent statesman as he was, instead of apostrophizing the financier in the hectoring tone he would certainly have adopted had the latter displayed any humility, he began quietly: "I desired to see you, M. Macrobe, to ask whether I had not been misinformed respecting the part you are said to have taken in the fatal duel of yesterday. It cannot surely be true that you, a man of order—a man on whom we rely—openly sided with a dangerous democrat against a gentleman known to be a trusted partisan of ours ? "

"I sided with M. Gerold because he was my friend," responded M. Macrobe calmly. "As for M. de Cosaque, or Panier, I am sorry he was a trusted partisan of your Excellency's, for it seems to me that the fewer of such hangers-on a respectable government tolerates, the better for its reputation in the eyes of honest people."

M. Gribaud's blood rose to his face, and he was on the point of giving a rough rejoinder; but, at the sight of M. Macrobe's impassive countenance, he controlled himself, and answered between his teeth: "I did not say a trusted partisan of *mine*, but of *ours*, by which I meant of the Government's and the Emperor's. You will probably allow that if his Majesty set store by M. de Cosaque, he had his reasons."

"I think we shall do better, perhaps, to come to an understanding, your Excellency," replied M. Macrobe, fixing his sharp eyes on the Minister's. "Whether his Majesty set store or not by M. de Cosaque, I am unaware; but in any case partisans of M. de Cosaque's kidney are not scarce in the market: the Government can find as many of them as it pleases by offering them their price. There are other men, however, whose support it is not so easy to obtain—men of talent, rank, means, and popularity, whose co-operation would be an element of strength to the Government. I presume your Excellency would not object if I enlisted such a recruit as that for our ranks?"

"To whom are you alluding?" inquired the Minister, wondering, but still sullen.

"Your Excellency has doubtless heard that M. Horace Gerold, whom you have termed a dangerous democrat, is heir to the ancient dukedom of Hautbourg, to a splendid estate conferring immense territorial influence, and to a moneyed fortune, which, by all accounts, must be considerable. M. Gerold is, besides, a man of talent, much esteemed by his party, and a little dreaded, if I mistake not, in Imperialist circles. What would your Excellency say if I brought this young man completely over to our party, if I induced him to assume his title, and to put both his landed influence and his own personal talents at the service of the Second Empire?"

It was now the turn of M. Gribaud to fix his eyes on his interlocutor.

"You think you shall be able to manage that, M. Macrobe?" he asked.

"I promise nothing," replied the financier; "but if the Government does not thwart me by heaping petty vexations on M. Gerold, I am confident of success."

"And you will bring Manuel Gerold and young Emile Gerold over too?" continued the Minister with a keen look.

"I cannot vouch for the younger brother; and to bring Manuel Gerold over would be impossible," answered M. Macrobe; "but Manuel Gerold is an old man, and in the course of nature must soon die. As to Emile Gerold, he is obstinate; but he will cease to be dangerous when his brother is with us—his party will never trust him."

"And of course for doing this you will require a reward?" observed the Minister, with more pungency than good taste.

"Naturally," rejoined the financier, with something of a sneer at the simplicity of the remark. "But I will ask for my reward at the fitting time and place. For the present, all I have to beg is, that your Excellency will see that M. Gerold is spared those fleabite annoyances which would be likely to sour him without doing the Government any good—I mean domiciliary visits, frivolous prosecutions, personal attacks in the semi-official press, and such like. Then again, I would make so bold as to request that judicial authorities be enjoined to evince more civility than they do at present. We have been before the Public Prosecutor this morning, and I assure your Excellency his tone was such as I was obliged to resent. He talked of the duel as a murder, which was at once ill-bred and unwise. A little civility never does any harm. It is a good saying that more flies have been caught with honey than with vinegar."

"Well, hark you, M. Macrobe," returned M. Gribaud, in the quick, matter-of-fact tone which was habitual to that statesman when he was striking a bargain with a person whose head he perceived to be as long as his own—"if you are working to bring young Gerold over to us, you shall not be meddled with—I promise you that much. Only, before disarming completely, we must have some sort of guarantee that you are not deluding yourself with false hopes. On what do you ground your expectations of success?"

"On the simple fact, that it is my interest to succeed," rejoined the financier, curtly; and this answer was so pregnant of confidence that it carried conviction with it. The Minister found nothing to reply, and the audience terminated. M. Macrobe, who had been kept standing all the while, retreated as he had come, with a slight bow, in which a little deference was mingled with a good deal of self-possession and no small dose of independence. M. Gribaud watched him go, and when the door had closed behind him, fell to rubbing one of his thick ears, thoughtfully, with a knotty forefinger, and muttered: "That fellow is a rogue to beware of. I wonder what his game is?" And, probably, speculations on this horny subject continued to harass the great Minister for the rest of the day: for M. de Beaufeuillet, the secretary, and the score of ambitious supplicants in the ante-rooms, soon had occasion to observe that his Excellency was in no better humour after his interview with M. Macrobe than he had been before it.

CHAPTER VI.

MADEMOISELLE ANGÉLIQUE.

IN proportion as the shares of the Crédit Parisien rose and the position of its Chairman became more brilliant, the world began to ask itself, with some curiosity, who the daughter of that gentleman would marry. The question was not altogether without interest, for it was reported that Mdlle. Angélique Macrobe would have ten million francs to her portion; and there were rumours that no less a person than the Prince of Arcola sought the honour of obtaining her hand.

However that might be, the young lady herself was to be seen every day in the Bois de Boulogne, surrounded by a glittering cavalcade of suitors, who pranced on various qualities of hacks round her showy barouche, bowed down to their saddlebows in offering her their homage, and sometimes went the length of pressing extremely tender billet-doux into her hand when they thought there was nobody looking. Of course Mdlle. Angélique's aunt sat by to act as chaperon, but that excellent lady, who could never forget the time when she had cooked the boiled beef which formed the staple article of M. Macrobe's daily banquets in the days when he was a struggling man, thinking a good deal more about the pence than he did now about the pounds—Mdlle. Dorothée was too much overawed by the dazzling presence of dukes and marquises to have any discernment left as to whether what these brilliant pretenders said and did was proper or not. When a handsome, lisping sprig of nobility bent over the carriage-door, she would muse in bewilderment how much that young man could spend a year for his yellow kid-gloves ; and when some enterprising *roué*, seeing her mild inquiring glance fixed on him, fancied she was watching to see whether he pushed things too far with her niece, he would be completely out of his reckoning. The poor lady was simply wondering what his Sunday clothes could be like since those he wore of a week-day were so fine.

As for Mademoiselle Angélique, she delighted, in her own inanimate way, in the life she was leading. To be dressed in light-blue silk and soft clouds of Valenciennes lace; to drive about in the barouche and see people stare at her; to have a box at the Opera, another at the "Italiens," another at every theatre when there was a new performance on: all this was better than being at school under those provoking nuns, who taught one when Clovis the First ascended the throne and when Clovis the Second descended from it. Then the gentlemen with the yellow gloves were amusing. They said funny things to make her laugh. That M. Gousset, for instance, called going to church the "baptism of new bonnets," and confession "clearing the conscience of its past sins in order to make room for those to come." The Prince of Arcola, to be sure, was a little grave: he didn't laugh so much. One of her school-friends had asked her whether it was true she was going to marry him. She didn't know; papa hadn't spoken to her about it.

If papa wished it, she should not mind. The Prince was always very kind to her, but she should like him to laugh a little more; it was more pleasant.

Every morning the butler of the Hôtel Macrobe brought in on a silver tray a whole pyramid of letters, burning acrostics, bouquets, and novels inscribed "with the author's compliments," all intended for Mademoiselle Angélique. The letters and acrostics were generally opened by M. Macrobe, and with the acrostics he seldom failed to light his cigar. The nosegays were stuck in vases, and the novels were handed over to Mademoiselle Angélique to read, if she cared to do so, which she never did. There were dozens of them ranged very neatly on the bookshelves of her boudoir, with the leaves cut of course (by a footman), so that an author, if he should chance to call and take up his own work for curiosity's sake, should never discover that it had not been perused. Mademoiselle Angélique did not like reading. "You have no idea how much they made us read at school," she would tell you, with a pretty, rueful expression on her bewitching face. She preferred drawing thatched cottages on a piece of white paper with a blue pencil; and when she was tired of that, she had a large red and green macaw on a gilt perch, whom she could tease with a silver bodkin.

She was precisely engaged in this last amusing occupation, when M. Macrobe invaded her bower one fine autumn morning some weeks after Horace Gerold's duel. M. Macrobe was always brisk, whether he had anything to say or not; but this time he *had* something to say.

At sight of her father Mademoiselle Angélique abandoned the bird of gay plumage and put up her face to be kissed.

"My pet, I have pleasant news for you," began the financier. "I mean to give a fancy dress and masked *déjeûner* in the country next month. I have hired a large villa and gardens for the express purpose. M. Girth, the *costumier*, will be here in an hour to show you designs for a costume—it must be a rich one: M. Gousset, whose taste is faultless, promised me to come and help me choose it. And—ahem! where is your aunt Dorothée?—Ha, there you are, sister. You will have to choose yourself a costume too. Blanche de Castille, I should think, or Catherine de Medicis would do very well.

"Oh, dear me, Prosper, you can't be thinking of putting me into fancy dress?" was aunt Dorothée's scared exclamation.

"Why not? Stuff and nonsense! Everybody must be travestied. You'll wear a mask too,—a velvet one with lace."

"Holy Virgin!" cried the poor lady, piteously. "And shall I be obliged to show my legs like those women at the play?"

"Your legs? No; what are you talking about? And don't say the play—it's provincial; say the theatre. Angélique, my pet, there will be no time to lose. As soon as you have chosen your dress, you must have it made up. I have called at Pochemolle's, and they'll send somebody over this morning to take orders for all the satin and velvet you may want. Girth will supply the needlewomen. Ah, and he'll have plenty to do, preparing dresses for this breakfast. I intend it shall be a fête such as has never been seen within living memory. There'll be a ball after it; and fireworks—a twenty thousand francs' worth. But we'll have only two thousand invitations—people shall go down on their knees for tickets. I have my reasons for all this. Eh, eh, it will be a magic sight!"

"Oh, papa, how nice!" exclaimed Angélique, in obedient ecstasy; and she began to wonder whether her costume would be pink or blue.

"Twenty thousand francs of fireworks—two thousand invitations! Gracious mercy! where's all that money to come from?" ejaculated aunt Dorothée, feebly staring at the chimney-piece.

But at that moment the butler opened the door and announced: "Monsieur Girth."

And the celebrated *costumier* was introduced.

He entered with grace, composed in his mien, irreproachable in his attire, easy in his salutation without being familiar. Behind him a satellite, with two immense folios, which were placed on the table. The strangest thing about Mr. Girth was that, holding the sceptre of fashion in the capital of fashion, he himself was a Briton born. You could pretty well guess this from his broad shoulders, light hair, and correctly-cut sandy whiskers.

"You keep good time, I see, M. Girth," said M. Macrobe, cheerfully.

"Punctuality is the politeness of tradesmen as of kings, sir," answered Mr. Girth, with a slightly foreign accent; "but I feared I was a few minutes behind my time, from having been delayed by the Duchess of Argenteuil — a wedding-dress for her Grace's daughter. I am also afraid I must hurry away in half-an-hour, to remit three dresses to a courier specially sent by the Empress of Austria."

Mr. Girth threw out these distinguished names without embarrassment, as if he had plenty more of the same grain ready to produce as occasion should serve him.

"Dear me," rejoined M. Macrobe. "I was in hopes you could have stayed until M. Arsène Gousset arrived to guide us in our choice. I expected him here by this time."

"Here *is* M. Gousset, papa," exclaimed Angélique.

And effectively that gentleman appeared, smiling and irreproachably dressed, coming up through the conservatory of camelias and ferns that adjoined Mademoiselle Angélique's boudoir.

He bowed to the two ladies, and shook hands with the financier. Mr. Girth made obeisance to him with a respectful inclination of the head.

"Well, Monsieur Girth, armed with your two manuals of elegance, I see. I have come to take a lesson in taste."

"Nay, sir. It is for M. Arsène Gousset to give, not to receive such lessons," answered the *costumier*, amiably.

"H'm! I don't know. I gave a description of a lady's dress in my last novel, and Madame de Masseline, one of your customers, told me I was at least six years behindhand with the fashions. I think she was right, for I lately saw, at one of the Embassies, a dress in which there was blue, green, yellow, and red, all mixed up together, somehow like in a Neapolitan ice. But they told me it was quite correct."

"May I ask at which of the Embassies, sir?"

"Your own: the English."

"Ah, yes: at the English Embassy they will do these kind of things," replied Mr. Girth, with a deprecatory shrug. "My countrywomen do not understand dressing, which is a pity, with their beauty. In England we have no middle class between those who don't dress and those who over-dress. Yet the science of costume is not difficult. Harmonize—there is the whole pith of it."

"Some pretty dresses here," murmured M. Gousset, turning over the leaves of the first album —"this one especially."

"Yes: a Francesca di Rimini, originally made for the Princess of Cleves. Her Serene Highness had been reading some Swedish romances, and desired to be costumed as "Margaret Waldemar." I had to use much diplomacy to persuade her Highness that she had neither the Northern complexion, nor the warrior-look necessary for the part. She had dark hair, and was sentimental. As 'Francesca di Rimini' she looked perfect. But that is the historical album. This is the fancy one, which will, perhaps, suit Mademoiselle better."

So the leaves of the fancy-book were turned over, and nymphs, goddesses, water-fairies, and cardinal virtues appeared in fascinating succession. At every page Angélique languidly exclaimed, "Oh!" and "Beautiful!" Aunt Dorothée, from hearing the prices called out, was quickly reduced to a state of intellectual coma, from which M. Gousset's suggested amendments—all of an expensive character—were not calculated to revive her.

The financier nodded his approval now and then, but deferred all practical decision to the novelist.

At last, by common consent, the choice was made to rest between a costume of Hebe and one of The Rising Morn.

"Something rich," hinted M. Macrobe.

"The Hebe would be simple," remarked the artistic Mr. Girth: "pearls, white silk and tulle, a little blue to give relief—perhaps a few flower-buds. The dress would not be more than twelve hundred francs. But I think the Hebe a little trite: I made three Hebes last winter season. The Rising Morn would be a much more imposing conception, and would harmonize exactly with Mademoiselle's rare beauty. Pale blue and white silk, with tulle as before, but arranged differently in diaphanous clouds, and the body much more *decolleté;* diamonds in profusion, to simulate dewdrops; gold powder in the hair—though, really, Mademoiselle scarcely needs it—and a tiara, with a rising sun in topazes and brilliants. To come up to my full idea in point of splendour, there should be a ten thousand guineas' worth of diamonds with this costume."

"Nothing to prevent it—nothing," answered M. Macrobe, enthusiastically.

"Well, if Mademoiselle decides on this costume, I think I can predict a success, especially by gaslight. It will be the finest thing seen since the 'Night' of the Duchess of Alba, though that was not finer."

Needless to say that Mademoiselle did decide upon that costume, and, hearing that the "person from M. Pochemolle's" had arrived, retired to give orders for all the quantities of silk and tulle which Mr. Girth was good enough to jot down on a paper.

The "person" had been shown into Mademoiselle's dressing-room.

Angélique hastened there, and found Georgette.

It should be mentioned that the two girls had been at school—or, rather, at convent—together some years before.

Angélique's father was then less than nobody; Georgette's was a respectable well-to-do tradesman: it was, therefore, Georgette who held the upper rank. The parts were now reversed, and perhaps, even in Angélique's naïvely serene temperament, lurked a spark of that good feeling which makes us so dearly love to patronize those who once have seen us lowly.

Anyhow she said, with a sweetly friendly smile: "Oh, Georgette, they never told me it was you: I wonder why they didn't. Do you know, I've been choosing a dress—at least, M. Gousset did for me—which is to have ten thousand guineas' worth of diamonds on it? It's a great deal, ten thousand guineas, don't you think so? How much is a guinea, I forget?"

Georgette smiled—a little sad smile it was, for the poor child did not look in mirthful mood—and said: "Are these the orders on the paper, Mademoiselle Angélique?"

"Yes, those are the orders, dear Georgette. Monsieur Girth wrote them; and he's going to send two needlewomen to work every day; but I am to try on before him, and the last touches are to be made by his foreman. Yes, I think that's what he said. But it seems odd—doesn't it?—for a foreman to be sewing ladies' dresses? Ah, but I'm forgetting you—you'll take a glass of Madeira and some cake to please me. I am going to ring for it. Then I'll show you over the house: I think you've never seen it. It's very big: I don't fancy I know my way all over it by myself."

"No, Mademoiselle Angélique, thank you. Please don't ring," said Georgette. "I must be home soon; but thank you very much, all the same."

"Oh, dear, but you must take something," exclaimed Angélique.

Then stopping, and gazing with a perplexed, rather astonished air at her friend, she said: "But, Georgette, you don't look as you used to—you've been ill, haven't you? You're quite pale; why didn't you tell me?"

And with an impulsive movement not common with her, she seated herself on an ottoman, drew Georgette to her, and kissed her.

"Tell me what it is, dear?" she said.

Georgette's heart was in that full state when the least drop of sympathy caused it to overflow. She burst into tears.

Angélique was much astonished and distressed.

"Dear me, I wish aunt Dorothée were here," she exclaimed. "I always go to her when I cry. But tell me, is it anything we can do for you? You were always good to me, you know, and you would never be sad if I could help it. I wish my head were better than it is; perhaps I might guess then without needing to ask you."

"No, no, it's nothing, Mdlle Angélique: it will pass away soon."

And Georgette made an effort to dry her eyes.

But it was only an effort, and it failed: so that when aunt Dorothée came up a few minutes afterwards to rejoin her niece she found the two young girls sobbing by each other's side—Georgette violently, Angélique helplessly and silently, from being unable to console her friend. The excellent woman was not long in adding her own tears to the group. But it was her mission in this life, poor soul, to boil beef and comfort the sorrowful: so after crying she gently pressed the afflicted girl to unburden her heart; and by degrees, by gentle questions, by dint of the confidence her kind worthy face inspired, she got at the truth. And that truth was the old, old story of a first love crossed. Georgette's father was bent upon marrying her against her will to a man she had never loved. He insisted upon it. Her mother, too, at first on her side, had ended by taking her father's, and they were importuning her so much that she knew she could not hold out longer. Besides, of what use was it to resist—she could never marry the man she loved? He would not have her; he was too high in the world, too much a gentleman to marry a poor girl like her. Yet she had once thought he loved her a little: it was an error. No, she would rather not tell his name. He had done nothing for which she could blame him. She would dry her tears and try to forget him. Well-meaning Georgette! this attempt was no more successful than the other. After drying her eyes she faltered again, and in this new gush of grief revealed that it was Horace Gerold she loved. . . . . .

An hour later, when she was gone, Angélique, her eyes still red, stole downstairs to look for her father. She had a scheme on her mind. The financier was alone in her boudoir examining a landscape he had bought the day before, for about a third of its value, of a jaded artist. He was deliberating where he should hang this, for the walls were pretty well covered as it was with good pictures purchased adroitly. His back was turned to the door.

She touched his arm.

"Oh, papa, I am so miserable, and I have come to ask you to do me a favour."

He laid down the picture a little surprised. This was the first time his daughter had ever asked him to do anything.

"It's not for myself, papa,—at least, if you do it, it will please me quite as much as if it were for me. It's for Georgette, you know, who was at school with me. She's been here this morning, and she says they want to marry her to a man she doesn't like. I think she said a commercial traveller. So I thought I'd come to you, though she told me not to do it, and ask you if something couldn't be done? If you spoke to her father, he would listen to you; and you might tell him—what she hasn't the courage to—that she loves a gentleman. I am not sure whether I ought to tell you his name;—I mean this gentleman's—but I will: it's M. Horace Gerold, the same whom you know. . . . ."

M. Macrobe, whose face had remained at first impassive, underwent a sudden elongation of countenance at the mention of Horace Gerold. He kissed his daughter on the forehead and turned abruptly on his heel.

"That's queer," muttered he to himself. "I wonder what it means. I suppose there's no new unpleasantness under these cards. H'm! Horace Gerold is not the man to marry a girl of that rank, even if he were twenty times in love with her; I know that much of him; still it's curious. Perhaps, there may be a way of turning this new affair to account. I must think about it?"

CHAPTER VII.

"THE FUTURE MADAME FILOSELLE."

"Ha, Gerold, how do you do? You have become quite a stranger here; but not for long, I hope?"

"Well, sir, my six months of disbarring will be over soon; perhaps I shall practise again then."

"Quite right. The Bar is the true career for talents fresh and vigorous like yours. By the way, how about your trial for that duel affair; are you committed?"

"I have just come from the *juge d'instruction's* closet; that is what brought me here this morning; but it seems I am to hear no more about the matter. I am discharged, as they say."*

---

* It is scarcely necessary to remind the reader that preliminary examinations are, in France, conducted *secretly;* and that the examining magistrate has unlimited discretionary powers.

"You owe that to your second, M. Macrobe, I suppose?"

"I think so. Perhaps a little, too, to the strength of my case. My antagonist was the aggressor; I acted in self-defence, and the jury could not but have acquitted me. The trial, however, would have afforded our counsel an opportunity for attacking the system of official journalism, and that I fancy would scarcely have suited the Government. They had more interest in hushing up the affair than we had."

Horace was replying to the barrister Claude Febvre, in the great hall of the Palace of Justice, where, as his interlocutor observed, he had for some time past become a stranger. He was still on the staff of the *Sentinelle,* but only waiting for the occasion to sever a connection which had ceased to be cordial, and which there appeared little likelihood of ever re-establishing on its old footing. Indeed the breach with Nestor Roche was widening rather than otherwise. The editor's confidence in his contributor was shaken. He tried not to show it, but the fact was patent, revealing itself in a host of small symptoms, not the least significant of which was the unusual latitude he allowed Horace as regards his articles. He never altered these articles now, never ran his pen through this or that sentence, pointing out with his gruff voice and friendly look, why he thought it wise to do so. The articles were printed as they came; and it is only fair to add, that if the editor had ever been troubled with apprehensions lest his headstrong young friend should drag the paper into trouble, all fears on this account were now definitely appeased. The duel, or rather the gathering intimacy with M. Macrobe which followed that event, appeared to have marked a new era in Horace's opinions, or at least in his style. He now wrote temperately, with an absence of all acrimony, sometimes even with a courtesy of expression which made the rougher republicans amongst his fellow-contributors quiver with astonishment. Not that he was less liberal: on the contrary, he was perhaps more so; but it was the easy, philosophical liberalism of the gentleman—the liberalism of the fortunate man who sees things through pink glasses, and begins to think that after all the world is not so black as it has been painted.

And how, indeed, could it be otherwise ? Every day added some new sweets to Horace's life. His walks along the Boulevards resembled triumphal processions. Distinguished men saluted him, great novelists and journalists nodded amicably to him as one of their own set; Bonapartist writers gave him a wide berth. When he went to the Opera, he must have been blind not to notice that women turned their opera-glasses in his direction —often kept them so turned a long time—and then M. Arsène Gousset, or the Prince of Arcola, would come down and claim to introduce him to Madame la Comtesse This or That, who desired to make his acquaintance. As Mr. Drydust remarked, it was flattering ; he knew what it was from having gone through it himself.

" Ah, *mon cher*," would add that eminent person, who was beginning to give him a good deal of his company, " take my word for it, extreme republicanism won't do. I've seen it act—went to

America on purpose to study it. The Americans have no opera of their own, no theatre, no novels worth mentioning, no pictures. And depend upon it these are the essentials of life."

" What are, novels or the opera ? "

" Both. Liberty should be not an end, but a means. You don't come into the world to put your vote into a ballot-box; you come to enjoy yourself. If you can't get the enjoyment without the vote, then agitate for the vote; but if you have the enjoyment, where is the use of voting ? "

" You mean that despotism which gives you operas and museums is the *ne plus ultra* of good government ? "

" Well, nearly. I adore despotism. Nothing great has ever been done without it. See this new Boulevard Malesherbes they are building; look at the Bois de Boulogne—two hundred million francs spent upon it within two years. Parliamentary government would never have done that for you."

" Then you must be very anxious to see the form of government in your own country changed."

"No; with England it is different. Freedom is necessary to the English temperament. We must have a great deal of freedom. But we are the exception."

Horace smiled; but these conversations, and a good many others of the kind, conducted by choice spirits like M. Gousset, were insensibly operating upon him. He laughed at the paradoxes he heard; would now and then take the trouble of refuting them; but like a man who has got into the habit of sipping absinthe, and, after finding his first glasses bitter, grows to like the acrid flavour: so now it rather amused him to hear the cynical witticisms of his new friends; and he more than once caught himself admitting—not aloud, but internally—that these agreeable fellows were much more genial company than the republicans pure he occasionally met. This was especially his train of thought on the morning he exchanged the few words in passing with the barrister, Claude Febvre. It was a clear, sunny day, his blood flowed prosperously in his veins, and the balminess of the air came as a welcome relief after an unusually gloomy hour or two passed the evening before in the society of some fervid Radicals. Never had these men—journalists and ex-politicians for the most part—shown themselves more iconoclastic and rabid. "Upon my word!" muttered Horace, as he descended the staircase of the Palace of Justice. "That may be liberalism, but if so, liberalism, like most other human inventions, would seem to be perfectible."

The streets were alive with that animation which buoyant weather begets. Cabs flitting by crossed each other with rapidity; on the tops of the omnibuses passengers talked and laughed; and the pink and yellow playbills on the kiosks gleamed singularly fresh and new. It was a day to be out and walking. Horace sauntered down the quays, stopping now and then to examine the curious collections of old prints and books exposed at the open-air stalls, which encumber the left bank of the Seine; but pausing more often to consider those wonderful pieces of rusty armour, those cracked plates of three-century-old china, and the japanned bowls of rare antique coins exposed in the windows of the bric-a-brac shops. He had just spent a minute thus profitably, and was turning to resume his stroll, when a small active pedestrian, in a showy waistcoat and loaded with a carpet-bag, ran almost into him, apologizing in the same breath for his awkwardness, and laying the blame on the narrow pavement. Horace bowed and was passing on; but the other, as if struck by his face, stopped, reddened a little, raised his hat suddenly, and said: "I beg your pardon. I believe I have the honour of addressing the Marquis of Clairefontaine — M. Horace Gerold? Pardon the liberty," he resumed immediately, "but I feel myself under an obligation: I owe you a debt of thanks, and I am thankful to have the opportunity of repaying it. My name is Filoselle—Hector Filoselle, at your service."

"M. Filoselle—yes, perfectly; I remember;" and Horace began to contemplate this gentleman with some interest.

"Yes, I owe you a debt of gratitude, Monsieur le Marquis—that is, Monsieur," said M. Filoselle, who was quickly regaining his self-possession,

"I am told you were good enough to employ your eloquence on my behalf. M. Pochemolle, my future father-in-law, has informed me of the circumstance. My future mother-in-law, you are aware, was at first opposed to the match. I have seen many mothers-in-law both in France and abroad, and have had occasion to notice that they are always opposed to something. Marriage, Monsieur le Marquis, would be a sacred institution but for mothers-in-law; when I am wedded I propose to keep mine at a distance. Mdlle. Georgette, my future wife, will, I have no doubt, subscribe to these views. Meanwhile, reciprocating my tender passion as she does, I am convinced that she entertains the same grateful feelings towards Monsieur as I myself."

Horace slightly bent his head without answering.

"I should have sought the opportunity of saying all this to Monsieur before; but the pursuit of business is engrossing; it has kept me away from Paris these last six weeks and will take me again into the country by the early train to-morrow. To amass money, M. le

Marquis, with the intention of bestowing it on the object of one's worship, is an occupation which has always seemed to me the noblest of all; and this reminds me that if Monsieur should want a few dozen of champagne, light and dry, vintage of '49; or a flute—rose-wood, with double silver stops, and a case to match, portable and convenient—he would find a profit in dealing with me preferably to with a retail house. I have another favour to ask, but this demand ought, perhaps, to be proffered by the future Madame Filoselle. However, if M. le Marquis would so far honour us as to be present at the ceremony, the date of which is not yet fixed, but shall be made known to M. le Marquis, he would be doing a gracious thing, for which he would be entitled to our sincerest thanks. Indeed, I may say, that by his presence M. le Marquis would be giving the final sanction to his own work; for if Hymen has happy days in store for me, I shall never be able to forget that it is to the Marquis of Clairefontaine that I owe it."

Was this true? Did Monsieur Filoselle owe

his prospective connubial bliss to M. le Marquis? One might have doubted it on seeing the pre-occupied and not over-pleased look on Horace Gerold's features as he moved away after this chance encounter. Why did things turn up in this way? Horace had resolved that he would think no more about Georgette, and he had really tried not to do so. He had even done more: he had avoided all occasions of meeting her; and once, when he was certain that she was not in the shop, he had entered, and resolutely undertaken a furiously long eulogy of M. Filoselle, whom he didn't know—all this with the view to mollifying Mdme. Pochemolle: in which object he had ended by succeeding. It is true that after this achievement he had retired, not particularly satisfied that what he had done was feeling, or even honest. But he wished to put away temptation, and the end in such cases generally appears to justify the means. One thing, however, he had neglected to do, and that the simplest of all: Why had he not removed? He did not know himself. He reasoned that the thing was not necessary, since Georgette herself would soon be married and gone. But, now, hearing M. Filoselle talk, it occurred to him that he had been unwise. It would have certainly been better to remove. He could not stand this commercial fellow coming many times and thanking him like that.

He walked home out of humour. A regret that M. Filoselle's employers had not sent that gentleman to sell their wares in the antipodes floated uppermost in his mind. Then he anathematized M. Pochemolle and all French fathers collectively who made a traffic of marriage. He wondered how Georgette looked now? It was a long time since he had seen her. Yes, weeks. What had she been thinking of him during all this while? She was indignant, of course; that must inevitably be, for women never view these things in the proper light. Still, he should be sorry that she should retain a lastingly bad opinion of him. He had acted for the best. Where would be the harm if he stepped in just to say a few kind words and make peace? She was definitely another's now; the attention could not be misconstrued.

He had reached the Rue Ste. Geneviève. He entered.

Mdme. Pochemolle was at her habitual place behind the counter. M. Pochemolle stood in the centre of the shop, receiving with respect a financial hint or two from M. Macrobe.

The latter accosted Horace, extending his hand.

"My dear young friend, I had called to tell you about this fancy fête of mine. It's got up mainly for you, you know."

Horace's eye roamed round the shop in search of Georgette. She was seated in a corner, and over the counter, talking to her and smiling, leaned a gentleman, fashionably dressed. They seemed tolerably engrossed in their conversation. "And," thought Horace, with a sudden and sharp pang at the heart, "their heads are very close together." This pang was not lessened when the stranger, turning round, showed his face. It was the Prince of Arcola.

CHAPTER VIII.

M. MACROBE "AT HOME."

M. MACROBE had determined that his fête should be a success; and, in so far as the preliminaries could augur, his wish appeared likely to be realized. M. de Tirecruchon, released from captivity, heralded the event in the *Gazette des Boulevards*. Mr. Drydust talked of it to his British readers, giving them full statistics as to the number of wax-candles that would be burned, the *menu* of the supper, and the price of the champagne—nothing inferior to Cliquot, twelve shillings a bottle. Suburban Clapham rejoiced over the feast as if it were going to be present there; the semi-detached villas in Camberwell, Battersea, Islington, and Chelsea, conversed anxiously about the entertainment during a fortnight beforehand.

But it was naturally in Paris that the coming revelry caused most sensation. The windows of the draper's shops along the whole length of the Boulevards and the Rue de la Paix bloomed out with flashing satins and rich-hued velvets, festoons of gold and silver lace, superb plumes, and countless stage accessories, amongst which, skilfully interspersed to catch the eye, shone gaudy designs of fancy dresses—mediæval queens, and Hungarian peasant girls, legendary amazons, and modern *vivandières*. Monsieur Louis, "Artiste Capillaire to the Court" (hairdresser, as we say in English), had got his "list" full—which meant that on the day of the fête he would start on his artistico-capillary rounds at six sharp in the morning, and terminate his labours towards midnight. Lucky the ladies who for a hundred francs' fee could obtain a quarter-of-an-hour of this gifted being's time! He drove up to the door in his brougham, raced up to Madame's dressing-room three steps at a time, expected to find Madame ready-seated before her toilette-glass, the maids in attendance, the combs, brushes, curling-tongs, and pots of *bandoline*, all in a row within hand-reach; and even then he would glare like a gladiator and stamp his autocratic foot if the maid was stupid— took a quarter of a minute, for instance, getting Madame's tiara out of the jewel-case, or in her hurry dropped a hair-pin. As for Mr. Girth, he was, of course, run off his legs.

There were no bounds, he would say, to the exigencies of ladies. If he called upon all who wrote to him he should never have a spare minute at his command. So he was really obliged to establish a rule. He would be at home at stated hours; other stated hours he would confine to calls; but his patronesses must please to understand that on no account could he ever devote more than half-an-hour to one consultation. It is not certain whether his patronesses understood this or not. Anyhow, their broughams extended in a three hundred yards' *queue* outside his door, and ladies who would not have waited five minutes to please their lawful husbands, sat, with the patience of saints, their two and four hours at a time to bide the good pleasure of Mr. Girth. Perhaps the only lady who, previous to the fête, was not called upon to undergo some ordeal of the kind was Mademoiselle Angélique.

As daughter of the host she was entitled to exceptional regard. Mr. Girth did himself the honour of waiting upon her personally once or twice a week, and she, apprised beforehand of his coming, awaited it with meditative anxiety, as we do the Doctor, or an R.A. who is coming to paint us. It was a scene not devoid of grandeur. Mademoiselle Angélique, attired in the as yet unfinished costume, stood motionless, with a cheval-glass to the right, another to the left, and a third in the background. Behind, but out of the line of sight, two attendant needle-women and a maid, silent and awe-struck. On a sofa, Mademoiselle Dorothée casting glances of resignation at the ceiling; and in the foreground, Mr. Girth, gloved, meditating, and impassive: throwing out curt orders to an aide-de-camp foreman, who deferentially consigned them to a note-book. Michael Angelo superintending the works of the cupola of St. Peter's; Lenôtre, planning the royal gardens of Versailles, were not more great and admirable.

To say that Angélique took pleasure in all this would be true, and yet her joy was not quite unalloyed. Her rich dress and the approaching fête were perplexing her a little. No doubt it was satisfactory to be informed that she would be queen of a pageant unsurpassed in splendour and unsurpassable; and to see the pretty eyes of her lady friends twinkle jealously as they examined her costume, and the ten thousand guineas' worth of diamonds to be tacked thereon, was a sensation of which any lady, however good at heart, will easily understand the sweets. But underlying these gratifying impressions, lurked a vague presentiment that this unusually brilliant festival had not been projected without some object in view—M. Macrobe, she knew, was not the man to invest twenty thousand francs in fireworks for the pleasure of watching coloured sparks fall—and somehow Angélique began to fancy that with her father's object, whatever it was, she herself might not be altogether dissociated. It must be confessed that her perspicacity scarcely went deeper than this. She thought, indeed, a little of the Prince of Arcola, wondered why, if he really intended marrying her, he did not propose sooner; but she was at a long way from guessing the truth, when the financier repeated to her for the fourth or fifth time:

"My pet, you must mind and be very civil to M. Horace Gerold, who will be present at the fête. You will find him a most amiable young man."

"Certainly," thought she, "I will be civil to M. Gerold," and she was very glad at having the opportunity of meeting him. As to his being an amiable young man, her father knew best, but it was not exceedingly amiable to act as he had done by Georgette. It is true that he was a rich and high-born gentleman, so they pretended, and that Georgette was a tradesman's daughter; but after all what did that matter? Had she not heard M. Gousset say often that a woman's rank was her beauty, that King Coph—Cophet-something had married a beggar-maid and that he had done quite right, for that the party honoured by this transaction was not the beggar-maid, but King Coph—himself—why then should not M. Gerold do as much? Georgette was not a beggar-maid: at school she used to carry off prizes which she —Angélique—could never manage to do; and she was pretty—oh yes, prettier far than any girl she had ever seen. Everybody declared so; even the Prince of Arcola, who had been to Pochemolle's the other day with her father, had come back quite enthusiastic about the young girl's beauty.

She wondered, in her mild, meek way, whether she could not try something to soften M. Gerold— he did not look like a very hard young man, and she was truly anxious to befriend Georgette. If her father had done what she wanted, the whole thing might no doubt have been settled by this time; but her father did not seem pleased at her interfering in the matter. He had kissed her quite abruptly and gone away, and the next time she had appealed to him, he had answered, impatiently: "Tut, tut, my pet, Georgette is a little goose, and you too."

She could not see why Georgette was a goose, though she had deliberated upon the matter gravely. It was not being a goose to cry because one had been jilted. Aunt Dorothée said it was a shame for gentlemen to steal away the hearts of young girls, that it was much more cruel and dishonourable than robbing money. Then Georgette was so gentle too! "Yes," thought Angélique, "I will try whether I cannot work upon M. Gerold's good feelings. I will take advantage of his presence at the fête to speak to him." This wise idea, which occurred to her after many days of reflection, she kept to herself; but every day the idea twined itself more tightly, like a strong shoot of ivy, round her usually inert imagination. Meanwhile, on the prettiest sheet of toned paper in the world, and with the tiniest gold pen extracted from a liliputian desk, she wrote to her friend "*not to be miserable*," drawing three lines under the word miserable, which, as connoisseurs in ladies' calligraphy are aware, means that there are three excellent reasons, if not more, why one should not be *miserable*. She added that she had got a plan for "*setting everything right*"—words underlined as before.

It is probable that if M. Macrobe had intercepted this affectionate communication on its way to the post and taken cognizance of its contents, he would have frowned, and with considerable vexation. But he was too busy now to see much of his daughter. Every spare hour he could snatch from business he spent at Marly in the villa he had hired, a noble residence with a beauteous park, in which a whole army of workmen were employed, erecting marquees, extemporizing terraces, and laying out parterres of costly flowers. Nothing was to be wanting to the completeness of the fête. In case of rain there were arrangements for covering in the entire grounds. Chalets, bright with paint and gilding, verdant with creeping foliage, had been run up here and there, and furnished with a luxury that could not have been excelled, had these ephemeral dwellings been destined to last permanently. To keep the grounds and line the approaches to the ball-rooms, a hundred men, attired as halberdiers, had been retained; and two hundred boys, dressed as pages of Francis the First, and selected for their comely looks, were to officiate as waiters. This part of the arrangements had been effected by a celebrated theatrical manager, expert in *mise en scène;* and the same enterprising genius had suggested that a hundred of the prettiest girls amongst the metropolitan *corps-de-ballet* should be recruited to act as *bouquetières,* and distribute to the guests flowers and bonbons. The programme might be altered according to circumstance, but for the present it was as follows: At four, the *déjeûner;* at six, the drawing of a tombola with valuable prizes; at ten, fireworks; after which the grounds were to be illuminated with an invention, then in its infancy, called "electric light;" masks were to be put on; and there was to be a ball, with supper and cotillon, lasting — until it pleased heaven to make the sun rise.

Small wonder that M. Macrobe was busy. He had long ago been obliged to relent from his original decision of only issuing two thousand invitations. No half-dozen post-bags could have contained all the letters he received cajoling, begging, entreating, raving for tickets. What made it difficult to refuse, too, was that there were a good many shareholders of the Crédit Parisien amongst the supplicants. These honest and importunate persons claimed the favour of an invitation as a sort of right, and they were delighted to hear of the fête, for it is evident that a chairman who has so much money to spend must be looking very closely after the interests of his shareholders. In fine, M. Macrobe had been obliged to increase the tickets to four thousand, without thereby greatly diminishing the number of those who in private declared they were being shamefully ill-used, and in public that they had never solicited invitations, not they, and that they certainly should not have gone to the party even if they had been asked. But M. Macrobe could afford to make light of these fox and grapes rancours. The essential point in his eyes was that all the personages of importance whom he had invited had accepted with alacrity, and that Horace Gerold—the most important of any—had, with perfect good-nature, entered into the spirit of the thing, and promised to come in costume. "So that's all right," muttered the financier; "and I think this seed-corn we are scattering will soon begin to fructify —barring accidents," added this prudent gentleman, who, in his calculations, always left a wide margin for contingencies.

At last the long-looked-for day of the fête arrived.

The evening before, Horace had attempted, without success, to induce his brother to accompany him. Emile had refused firmly but gently; alleging no reason, however, save the somewhat indefinite one, that he should probably be busy. Horace had hired for three hundred francs a magnificent costume in the fashion prevailing under Henry II. (of France). It was white satin slashed with cerise; a short mantle of white velvet profusely embroidered with silver fell over the shoulders, a silver-hilted sword in cerise velvet sheath hung by his side, and a flat bonnet with white plumes fastened with an aigrette of diamonds adorned the head. Now, it may be weakness, but when we have attired ourselves in a garb of this sort, and are surprised by a friend contemplating ourselves in a glass, we expect to be complimented on our appearance, otherwise we look foolish. Horace felt so when Emile, entering unexpectedly, just as he had put on a pair of red-heeled shoes and was watching the effect of them, said gravely: " Oh! I beg your pardon, I see you are engaged."

"Engaged! no," exclaimed Horace, reddening with some confusion. "Come in, man, what is it you want to say?"

"I was going to write to Brussels to-day. Have you any message I can send?"

"My love, of course. But what are you going to write about?" asked Horace, wishing he had got his black coat and trowsers on instead of these silk stockings and this sword.

"Well, you know, I received a letter yesterday:— and, by the way, what am I to answer about the passage that concerns you?"

Horace sat down on his bed and played moodily with his bonnet.

"How am I to say?" answered he in a vexed tone. "The whole thing is absurd and calumnious. Some of those Republicans of Brussels have been telling my father that they hear I am keeping loose company, and am turning renegade; and he feels pained. Tell him it is not true; and you might add that it is only Republicans who would be capable of inventing such trash; for I am sure I begin to think with Jean Kerjou, that we shouldn't be happy in our party if we didn't perpetually accuse one another of treachery."

"And what am I to say about M. Macrobe?" proceeded Emile quietly.

"M. Macrobe is my friend," replied Horace in an impatient voice. "I've told you so already, and think you might spare me the trouble of repeating it. Write to my father that he is misinformed about the man. Thank God, our father is not cut out of the same wood as his brother Republicans; he has the soul of a gentleman, is just and generous. He can require nothing more when I say that I answer for M. Macrobe's honour on my own."

"On your own honour, brother?" answered Emile doubtfully. "You are not surely in earnest; for if you really went bail for this man's honour, Horace, how could *I* hold out any longer? You cannot think that I would continue to suspect the man if I thought you convinced of his honesty."

"But why *do* you suspect him?" rejoined Horace with irritation. "What is the meaning of this mania of yours for suspecting people, you who used to be such a good fellow, and never spoke ill of a fly? It seems to me that it is you who are being spoiled by bad company—that of these envious, bilious demagogues whom they tell me you frequent. What has M. Macrobe done to you, come, tell me that; and what has he done to me? Why, since I have come across his path he has done nothing but repay me good for evil—had he been Job himself he could not have evinced more longanimity. I begin by vilifying him in a court of justice—he holds out his hand to me and asks me to dinner; I cut him—he takes my part when I am publicly insulted, and risks imprisonment by abetting me in a duel; he knows I am a Republican, that is a foe to his party, and he good-naturedly asks my advice about distributing twenty thousand francs to the people of our clique who may have suffered during the revolutions. Frankly, what can be his object? I am no great man that he should have any interest in currying favour with me. I am a poor devil without fortune or title, with only a rag of popularity at my back, which a day has made and which a day may take away. M. Macrobe, on the contrary, is a millionaire with more power than a cabinet minister. It would be both presumptuous and arrogant to pretend that there can be anything else but condescension on his part in treating me in the way he does."

The blood rose to Emile's habitually pale face.

"Well, Horace, this is the last time I shall ever speak about M. Macrobe, then," said he, with the slight hectic cough which excitement of any kind generally brought on. "I will not promise to like the man," added he with an effort. "But your good word is a passport—to, at least, my respect. For your sake I will try to forget what I had heard and believed about M. Macrobe."

And he held out his hand—a white, thin hand it was, and feverish.

"Why won't you go to this fête with me?" asked Horace, still dogged.

"No: don't ask me to do that," pleaded Emile, shaking his head. "To begin with, I should not make a very lively guest; and I hardly think I could afford the expense. Besides, you see it is too late now. I fancy this is the concierge come to tell you that your carriage is waiting."

It was no longer Georgette who ran up on these sorts of errands now. The concierge, cap in hand, informed "Monsieur" that a gentleman in a landau with postilions was down below, "dressed like in carnival time." The person meant was the Prince of Arcola, who had arranged to call for Horace and give him a lift. Horace put on his glittering bonnet, wrapped himself in a flowing cloak of white cashmere, and descended.

Never since the days of the Grand Monarque, when high court and revelry were held there, had the shady groves of Marly resounded with the echoes of such a festival. It was an event to be remembered evermore by the inhabitants, and to be narrated some eighty years hence by the youngest of them as a reminiscence of how men lived and caroused under the notorious Second Empire. A troop of mounted municipal guards, their steel helmets and breastplates flashing in the sun of a cloudless sky, had been lent by the Prefect of the Seine to act as guard of honour. Picked men, with flowing moustaches, slung carbines, and clinking sabres, they swept up the Grand Avenue at a fast trot half-an-hour in advance of the first carriages; then, having reached their destination, turned and separated—half forming themselves into a glittering semicircle round the park gates, the others starting off by twos to occupy strategical points down the road, and silently point the way to doubting coachmen. Simultaneously a hundred members of the Parisian police took up their position at equidistant spaces of twenty yards on either footway to keep back the curious, and see that the stream of vehicles flowed by uninterrupted. Magnificent policemen these, with cocked hats, straight swords, white gloves, folded arms—men you would have taken for officers in any other country. Then the carriages began to appear, first singly, then two or three almost abreast, as if racing; then one after another, settling gradually into a gorgeous slow-moving procession that seemed never to end, tapering and glimmering far into the distance, out of the reach of sight, like the trail of a starry meteor. The harness of the horses jingled, the hoofs of the noble animals pawed the ground impatiently, large flakes of foam dropped from the furbished bits, coronet after coronet, 'scutcheon after 'scutcheon flashed by on shining panels, and, every now and then, down the whole line there would be that ten minutes' dead stop, which acts on the nerves of fair occupants of broughams, and evokes from the powdered gentlemen on the box such doleful replies as this: " Impossible to move faster, Madame la Marquise; there are more than two hundred carriages ahead of us."

But if the scene without was sufficiently imposing, what language can be used to paint the spectacle within the grounds? Such a sight needs more than a pen. Tents of purple vellum and gold, gilt awnings ablaze with silken streamers; squads of radiant girls with pyramids of flowers piled up in vase-like baskets. On plats of emerald grass, and under the spreading shade of giant oaks, rich carpets and velvet cushions spread out to invite repose; and trenching on the marble whiteness of terraces, the drooping folds of blue, scarlet, and orange draperies. If anything, the eye had too much of colour, and turned with relief to the cool fountains, which threw up their waters in columns of spray, and splashed so musically in the round deep basins. Fair forms leaned over these basins, dipped their hands in, and filled the air with tinkling laughter. And these silvery sounds formed a melodious interlude to the strains that issued from the open orchestra pavilions, around which, eddied and flowed a festive crowd revelling in garbs of every variety of fashion, richness, and tint.

"Upon my word it seems to be a success," said the Prince of Arcola to his companion as they passed together into a sumptuous reception-marquee where a master of the ceremonies, who looked cut out of a picture by Titian, took their cards.

The master of the ceremonies bowed low before them and two pages in green and gold stepping forward, relieved the one of his white cashmere cloak, the other of a blue roquelaure that concealed a costume in violet velvet, of the time of Henri IV.

CHAPTER IX.

YOUNG CANDOUR, OLD SUBTLETY.

"Now here you are, that's right, and I am going to tell you who all the people are," cried Mr. Drydust, laying hold of Horace's arm as soon as he caught sight of him.

Mr. Drydust figured as a Scottish chieftain, presumably Rob Roy, and his intelligent brow disappeared under a bonnet of warlike dimensions. But he was none the less affable. Slightly embarrassed by a giant claymore from the hilt of which he was afraid to trust his left hand very far, his pace was perhaps less rapid than usual, but he still made excellent play with the hand remaining to him, and waved it about gracefully and easily to give effect to all he said: "Now see," said he; "this is true ease—the ease of an age when men understood costume, and fashioned it so as to give free play to all the limbs. I always feel fettered when I wear a frock coat—pardon, Madame" (Mr. Drydust had tripped up over his claymore), "but in this, one is at home. Aha, there is my friend Catfeesh Pasha; I'll introduce you. I declare this is like the Corso of Rome in Easter week; one meets everybody one knows."

So one did. All Paris was present. Not in truth the Paris which eminent foreigners would have comprehended in that title. One might have searched the whole grounds through without finding a single one of the men whose presence here below will be remembered a hundred years hence. But the Paris of the Second Empire was there, a throng of senators, ministers, deputies, stock-jobbers, patchouli-novelists, eau-de-rose journalists, and the gayer spirits of the Corps Diplomatique, all in short who would consent to clothe themselves in the garb of departed centuries and stalk about thus clothed for the amusement of the community. M. Macrobe had allowed of no exceptions in this respect: modern attire had been pitilessly excluded, and Horace met, within a space of five minutes, a cabinet minister dressed as a Turk, a councillor of state habited as a Jew pedler, and an envoy extraordinary and minister plenipotentiary disporting himself very successfully as a Cochin-China fowl.

In these sorts of things it is highly essential that the guests should not be thrown too much upon their own resources, but that there should be a few sportive minds, to leaven the lump, play the fool a little, and keep the merriment from flagging. M. Arsène Gousset had undertaken this part. He was the presiding genius of the fête. Assisted by M. de Tirecruchon, some young journalists, and three or four artists, he darted about from group to group organizing quadrille parties, introducing people one to another, and seeing that there was an endless flow of champagne. He had also composed a jocular *Gazette des Masques*, which, printed in gold on white satin, was distributed broadcast by him and his acolytes with piping cries such as newsvendors utter.

Horace would have been glad to sit down somewhere, whence he could have seen without being himself observed; but this would not have tallied with the plan of his host, which was to make him an actor in, not a mere spectator of, the pageant. M. Macrobe had instructed swift messengers to bring him immediate intelligence of Horace's arrival, and the latter had scarcely had time to accustom his eyes to the novel show around him, when the financier, transformed into a Jacques Ango, (famous merchant of Dieppe who threatened to make war upon Portugal at his own cost, in the reign of Francis I.) accosted, welcomed, and drew him away with Mr. Drydust to the *déjeûner* tent.

There Mademoiselle Angélique was holding her court, amidst a dense circle of worshippers, transfixed with admiration. Flattering murmurs circulated on all hands: Horace himself was fairly dazzled. Certès, the great M. Girth had triumphed. Nothing could have been more beautiful, more enchanting than this young girl of angelic loveliness, dressed in the graceful disguise of the Rising Sun. Her round white arms were bare, except where glittering bands of jewels encircled them, her rich hair fell in golden cascades over her snowy shoulders, the sun of brilliants that crowned her fair brow blazed like the fiery orb it represented, and the child herself, intoxicated by the incense of praise, enlivened by the music, the wine, the festivity, the compliments, glowed with an animation which heightened her beauty a hundred-fold.

"You must cater for my daughter," said M. Macrobe, leading Horace forward, and introducing him.

And, noting the ill-concealed look of envy on the countenances of some of the suitors he was then ousting, Horace could not avoid the reflection that, perhaps, indeed he was a man to be envied.

The tent was rapidly filling, for the signal had gone forth that the *déjeûner* was served, and fancy costume is no deterrent to appetite.

Horace led Angélique to one of the numerous tables spread in view of this tardy luncheon or early dinner. He was more or less the cynosure of a group of ladies, not indisposed to flirt with him on the strength of his reputation as a "lion;" but his matchless partner engrossed him, and she, to reward his assiduities, smiled, talked, and occasionally fixed her eyes upon his with a curious expression at once pleased and confiding, which, devoid of fatuity as he was, sent the blood to his head, and caused his heart to palpitate.

M. Macrobe, from whose watchful glance none of these signs, however slight, escaped, smiled to himself with contentment. He was standing with the Prince of Arcola.

"Well, mon prince," he said, "have you forgiven me for taking you to see that pearl of price—that bewitching Mademoiselle Georgette—the other day? I remember you said it was doing an ill-service to show you a face that would inevitably remain fixed in your memory, and, perhaps, trouble your peace."

"Did I say that?" replied the Prince, with an embarrassed laugh. "One says those things, you know, without meaning them. A handsome statue, a striking picture, creates an impression which one at first thinks lasting, but which wears off."

"To be sure. But Mademoiselle Georgette is a very striking picture;—at least, I know of some one who was considerably smitten in that quarter."

"Who?" asked the Prince, quickly; not noticing that, at this vivacity, which somewhat belied his previous indifference, M. Macrobe's eyelids slightly twinkled.

"That would be telling tales out of school," laughed the financier. "Still, mon prince, as a secret between you and me, the admirer was young Gerold. You know he lives in the same house as this handsome statue."

The Prince changed colour a little. It did not look as though the news much pleased him.

M. Macrobe, to repair matters, took his arm, and presented him to the fascinating daughter of an American citizen, Cincinnatus Jickling, Esq., whose ambition was to crown a long career of democracy and drysalting by allying himself to some one with a title. Mr. Jickling was stirred to the depths of his republican heart on seeing Miss Jickling escorted to the breakfast-table by an authentic prince.

Amidst the popping of champagne-corks, the clattering of plate, the running to and fro of sprightly pages, carrying silver trays loaded with choice viands or eccentric-shaped flagons, Horace pursued his attentions to Angélique. When the banqueting was at length over, she accepted his arm, and they issued on to the lawn.

"How refreshing the air is," she said. "But we must sit down—or shall we go to one of those châlets? They look so nice and cool."

So they turned their steps towards the châlets, which were deserted—the stream of wassailers being directed towards another part of the grounds, where the Tombola was to be drawn.

M. Macrobe, who saw them walk alone, was careful not to disturb them. He had now mated himself with an English dowager—the Lady Margate—who had seen the Eglinton tournament, and was regaling him with her recollections of that historic event. He led off her ladyship, and charmed her with his good-humour, his perfect manners, and admirably-genial deference. "A most becoming Frenchman," was her ladyship's unuttered verdict.

Yet, if M. Macrobe could have divined the motives of his daughter for enticing Horace to the châlet, it is not so sure that Lady Margate would have been captivated by his demeanour. It is probable that he might have earned the reputation of being a very distraught and ill-tempered Frenchman.

As we have said, Angélique had come to the resolution that she would help Georgette. This was the first time in her life that the idea of helping any one—or even the possibility of doing so—had ever occurred to her; but, from the very fact of its novelty, the determination had taken firm hold of all her faculties, absorbing her energies, and monopolizing her thoughts. There are no resolutions so deep as those which have been a long time taking root. She had turned the matter over waking, dreamed of it sleeping, and ultimately had resolved that, cost what it might, she would do such and such a thing on a certain day.

As we must never make men and women braver than they are, perhaps one ought to own that, at the moment of putting her scheme into execution, she was not a little emboldened by the two or three glasses of Madame Veuve Clicquot's vintage which she had sipped. Anyhow, they were no sooner seated than, with the amazing courage of innocence and inexperience, looking up into Horace's face, she said :

"I am sure you must be very good."

"Good?" replied he, disconcerted. "Are men ever good?"

"Yes, I think you are. I have heard gentlemen speak about you: they said that, though rich, you were a friend of the poor, and gave all your money to them. It seems to me that if I were a man I should like to be like that. I see many gentlemen who pass their lives in trying to amuse themselves; they do not appear to me so happy as you. Only, if I were a man, and anybody loved me

I think I should perceive it, and I should not despise the love; for, you see, we women have nothing to give but our hearts, and when we have bestowed that, if we do not get another heart in return, our lives are dark and miserable ever after."

Horace sat not knowing what could be the meaning of this. Was it a declaration? He felt what is called queer. The incomparable beauty of the girl who was addressing him, the solitude, the strangeness of the situation, all combined to form one of those passes in which precipitate men do foolish things. Luckily his emotion deprived him for the moment of utterance, and thus saved him from ridicule.

"You look astonished," pursued Angélique artlessly; "but what I say is true. Men are strong, and should have pity on the weak. A woman's love may not be much in the estimation of a man, but if they only knew what tears and suffering it costs, I think they would be too generous to leave it unrequited. I know people say that marriages should be between persons of the same rank and having like fortunes: but do you really think this is the only way to become happy? Is affection quite worthless, unless it have armorial bearings on it like one's dinner-spoons?"

Altogether on the wrong tack, and growing much more excited than was prudent, Horace seized Angélique's hand.

"Can you suppose," he said gallantly, "that any sordid considerations would stand in the way of my marrying a woman who gave me her heart?"

She abandoned her hand to him without mistrust; but in a tone of wondering remonstrance: "Then why do you not marry Georgette?" she asked.

"Georgette!" he exclaimed, suddenly releasing her hand.

"Why, yes: of whom else could I be speaking?" replied she simply. "I learned your secret,—at least, it would be truer to say that my aunt and I wrung it from poor Georgette, for she would never have told it us of her own accord. But she is very unhappy, Monsieur Gerold, believe me—so unhappy that I thought I would tell you this, for I said to myself: 'It is impossible M. Gerold can be aware of the pain he is causing.' Georgette is my old school-friend, you know; we were at the convent together; and she was a much better and cleverer girl than I;— oh yes—and there is not a nobleman in the world but might marry her without derogating."

The position was perplexing. A man always plays a rather silly part if he has been supposing without reason that a woman is making love to him. Horace felt neither more nor less abashed than most men feel under such circumstances. Yet Angélique, in pleading for her friend, was so naïvely eloquent, her voice bore the accent of so much womanly kindness, that he was touched. Had her design been to win him to herself, by a comedy adroitly played, she could not have succeeded more completely. Perceiving that she had not been thinking in the least about him, he began, with man's unfailing instinct, to think about her.

He hesitated a moment; then, drinking in her truly uncommon beauty with his eyes, he said, "Mademoiselle, my conduct has been misrepresented if you have been told that I have trifled with the affections of the young lady you mention. Had I loved, there are no considerations of rank or fortune that would have dissuaded me from marriage. But to marry without love, or with love existing only on one side, would be folly; and I assure you that until this day my heart was free. Yes," added he, becoming quite serious, whilst his voice grew more impassioned, " until I came here two hours ago I never knew what love was. The aims of my life were selfish: they tended to my own advancement only, and I had never contemplated associating any woman with my destiny. But from this day"—and he fixed his eyes with an intent gaze on her—" I have a new ambition,—one that will blend itself with and sanctify all my other aspirations—and this ambition it is you alone that will have the power to fulfil it."

He rose, looking at her with a new glance full of

love and meaning; and before she, in her surprise and distress, had found a word to say, he was gone.

Whilst this was taking place in the châlet, the world was enjoying itself at the drawing of the tombola, and Mr. Drydust was explaining to the Austrian ambassadress wherein this tombola, which was a plain lottery, differed from the Italian tombolas—an exposition to which her Excellency listened with as much good-nature as though her husband had never been civil governor of Milan, and specially occupied during ten years of his life in superintending the Austro-Lombard lotteries. At every moment there was enthusiasm and clapping of hands, as a spirited lady, perched aloft on a platform and turning a wheel-of-fortune, drew out a ticket and proclaimed a prize; which M. Gousset (capital make-up as a court-buffoon), or one of his staff, instantly fetched from behind a curtain and handed, with compliments, to the owner of the winning number. As a general rule, these lotteries are not a boon. One gets pen-wipers which one doesn't want, or paper-cutters which embarrass one the whole evening; but M. Macrobe had ordained this on the same grand scale as the other arrangements. He had simply invested five thousand guineas in jewellery, and not the least pleasing feature of his triumph was the amazement of his lady-guests, who, examining the lockets or brooches they had drawn, discovered them to be real gold! The sharpest of money-men find it difficult to steer clear of snobbishness.

But amidst this riot and jubilation a slinking somebody, draped in a Venetian cloak and wearing a black mask, was wandering about looking for the host. As the day was waning, and it was part of the programme that masks should be assumed at dusk, the Venetian-cloak gentleman soon found his example followed, which appeared to make his researches more difficult, for he more than once stopped and fixed on the wrong man, interrogating him first, and then apologizing. At last he lit upon M. Macrobe, who had just watched his daughter and Horace leave the châlet at a few minutes' interval, both flushed and pensive, and was quietly radiant.

"M. Macrobe," said the mask. "I thought I should never find you."

M. Macrobe started at the voice.

"Is it possible—can it be your Excellency?" he exclaimed. "This is an honour I dared not have counted on."

"Well, well," muttered M. Gribaud—for it was he—"my wife and my daughter were here: you had been good enough—hem—to send them an invitation, so I thought I would just come in like this:" he glanced deprecatingly at the cloak that covered his legs and gave a slight shrug.

"Your Excellency could not have conferred a greater favour—but let me lead you to the refreshment tent—you must be exhausted."

"No, no, thank you! By the way, if you have a mask, too, it might be as well to put it on; we shall be the less noticed."

M. Macrobe was not sorry to cover his face. Interviews with Monsieur the Minister Gribaud were often severe tests to physiognomical impassiveness. He knew his Excellency well enough to be certain that this unexpected visit was no mere act of amiability, but must have some business motive at the bottom of it.

"I have come because I had something to say on a matter that concerns us both," began the statesman, leading the way to a retired avenue. "You are still getting on well with young Gerold?"

"Your Excellency can see him yonder," answered M. Macrobe, turning. "There to the left, in the cerise and white, talking to a lady—Mdme. de Margauld."

"Yes, I see him. Humph! how the boy has grown since I knew him. Well, M. Macrobe, you remember the conversation we had some time ago about this young man . . . . ?"

"Assuredly; and your Excellency must have noticed that the confidence I then expressed was not unfounded. Compare the political attitude of M. Horace Gerold now, and his attitude six months ago."

"He still gives us a great deal of trouble with those newspaper articles of his."

"I did not guarantee immediate results. Your

Excellency will recollect my stating that the conversion would need a certain time; yet even in these newspaper articles, you must have remarked a daily increasing moderation."

"Moderate criticisms, M. Macrobe, are not those which give least annoyance," answered the Minister phlegmatically. "Still, I grant there is a change; what I have now to propose is an arrangement that may do a great deal at a single stroke. M. Chapoteau, the member for the Tenth Circumscription of Paris, died this morning."

"Which renders a seat vacant."

"Yes, and one it will be difficult to fill as we should like. That poor Chapoteau was a fool, but he made an excellent member. He was elected immediately after the *coup-d'état*, when people were still frightened, and he never gave us a minute's bother. But it would be nonsense hoping to get such a one elected again. People have got over their fright now, and they will be for electing some Radical just to spite us; it's always the same story with these Parisians. However, if you can answer that young Gerold will come over to our side by-and-by, it might be worth while putting him forward and letting him carry the seat, which he might do, popular as he has become."

"But how could the Government help him? Horace Gerold would not accept an official candidateship; neither, did he accept it, could he hope to win the seat, for his popularity would collapse on the spot."

"You don't quite follow me," answered M. Gribaud, with some impatience. "My suggestion is that you should induce young Gerold to stand as opposition candidate. We, of course, shall have our official candidate, and we will do our utmost to get him through; but failing the possibility of that—and I repeat, I don't think it is possible—our agents will receive instructions to give Gerold all the occult assistance they can. And supposing there should be several opposition candidates, and that a *ballotage* should be necessary by reason of the division of votes; then, on the second day's polling, our candidate shall withdraw in Gerold's favour, and so make the seat safe for him. All you will have to do is to prevent the young fellow from entering into any league with his brother opposition candidates."

There was a silence. M. Macrobe mused a moment.

"I will be frank with your Excellency," he said, at last. "I am rather afraid to adopt this plan. If it were certain that within a given time of his entering the house, Horace Gerold would cross over to the Government benches, the scheme would be a good one; but I greatly fear that if once elected as an opposition candidate, he would remain faithful to his party ever after. Gratitude in the first place, and in the next the pride of occupying an absolutely unique position—that of sole liberal member in a house full of Bonapartists—would combine to revive his republican sympathies, and so undo all the work we have been so patiently pursuing of late. But there is another way in which it strikes me this election can be turned to account in bringing young Gerold over more rapidly to our camp." M. Macrobe paused, and threw his eyes round him to make sure there were no eaves-droppers. "We will prevail upon Gerold to stand as opposition candidate, your Excellency; but we must contrive to get his election defeated by the Radicals. Let the Government press have orders to combat him, courteously; on the other hand, let there be stirred up against him a few of those Radicals who have affinity with the Préfecture de Police, and let these fellows be incited to assail him with all the ranting violence and calumnious abuse with which their pleasant vocabulary is stored. They might be licensed to start a paper on purpose to attack him, and furnished with the necessary funds. This would disgust Gerold. He is extremely sensitive; he shrinks from blackguardism, and the more signal the courtesy shown him by his Bonapartist opponents, so much the more would he writhe under the low insults of his own party. If he lost his election through their doings, it would be all up with the connection. I should not be surprised to see him snap it there and then, and desert over to us in a dudgeon with arms and baggage."

His Excellency M. Gribaud passed his knotty hand over his chin. The project of M. Macrobe evidently tallied completely with his own ideas as to how an election ought to be carried on under the reign of Universal Suffrage. He saw no flaw in it. He approved.

"The only thing is about the vacant seat," muttered he. "Who will have it?"

"Not unlikely your official candidate," answered M. Macrobe, smiling. "If Gerold breaks with the radicals he will, probably, resign in favour of the Bonapartists to mark his utter contempt for the party he abandons. Then by this election your Excellency will have killed two birds with one stone—kept the seat in the Corps Législatif for the Bonapartists, and won over a dangerous adversary."

It was some time before these two pillars of the political and financial worlds separated. As their mutual esteem for each other increased by the disclosure of kindred sentiments, they continued to converse, broaching a variety of topics, and taking one another's moral measure. When

M. Macrobe was again free, night had set in. Signor Scintilli, the pyrotechnician, had discharged his twenty thousand francs' worth of fireworks—the most goodly blaze ever seen—and the maskers had all retreated from the night-air into the brilliantly-illuminated saloons where the ball was to take place. The financier hurried across terraces and up staircases in his sable-gown and gold chain. He was bent upon finding Horace at once, and obtaining from him a promise to stand at the election. Wine, music, and the revelry aiding, it was presumable the young man would be more accessible to the counsels of ambition, more inclined to view his chances with a sanguine eye, than in a soberer mood to-morrow. But first M. Macrobe wished to see Angélique for a single moment, and discover by a passing question whether Horace had committed himself to any proposal.

The ball had commenced, and the financier stood regarding it from the threshold of the room. Everybody was masked, and, as a consequence, everybody was behaving as he or she would not have done had their features been unveiled. The distinguished plenipotentiary, dressed as a fowl, was kicking his legs in the air in a style that would have secured his immediate ejection from Mabille. A quadrille composed of official deputies and senators' wives, figuring the devil, a monk or two, some historical dames, and a clown, were going through evolutions, which excited shrieks of interminable laughter from a surrounding ring of noble and illustrious spectators. Mr. Drydust, long ago severed from his claymore, and with his arm encircling the waist of a Russian princess, was performing all his steps Scotch-reel wise, and flinging his manly limbs about him like the branches of a tree, tempest-tossed. M. Gousset had so thoroughly entered into the spirit of his part that one would have taken him purely and simply for one of the loose characters of his own novels. M. Macrobe caught sight of Angélique seated and fanning herself. She had just been dancing with the Prince of Arcola, and, on account of the heat, had for a moment taken off her mask. Her aunt Dorothée, utterly unrecognisable and weird to witness as Catherine de' Medici, was beside her. Poor woman, she looked like a worthy soul from the upper world fallen by accident into pandemonium.

"Well, my pet, is your card pretty full?"

"Oh, papa, look!" she said. "I don't know how I shall ever keep all these engagements."

In truth, the card was full from the first dance to the twenty-second inclusive. An instant's survey showed M. Macrobe that Horace's name was not down.

"Have you danced with M. Gerold?" he asked carelessly.

Angélique blushed scarlet.

"M. Gerold never asked me," she said, fanning herself more rapidly and speaking shyly.

M. Macrobe knew all he cared to know.

"The courtship has begun," he muttered gaily; and he made for a corner of the room where Horace, easily discernible, though masked, was handing the fascinating daughter of Cincinnatus Jickling, Esq., back to her seat after—as she prettily termed it—"going the pace" with her.

Five minutes later there were two happy men in the room—M. Prosper Macrobe, who had obtained his promise and been thanked into the bargain with a sudden and earnest effusion of gratitude that had surprised him; and Horace himself, who, animated with the whole day's proceedings, the wine, the lights, the dance, was saying, with beating pulse and glistening eye: "Deputy at twenty-five! I shall not have a fortune to offer her, but I can make myself a name: and then, perhaps, her father will not refuse his consent. That man seems to be my guardian angel."

CHAPTER X.

"LE LION AMOUREUX."

THE presence of the Prince of Arcola in M. Pochemolle's shop—a novel incident on the day when Horace first beheld that nobleman there—had gradually become an event of daily occurrence. M. Macrobe knew what he was about when he brought the Prince to see Mdlle. Georgette. The Prince, to his weakness for horses and heraldry, added a third more artistic weakness for women. It was not the weakness of a debauchee, but the highly-cultivated and epicurean worship for what he deemed the fairer and incomparably better half of creation.

The Prince of Arcola was one of those gentlemen who would be all the happier for having some object to their lives. To be sure, he cherished an ambition, which was to win the French Derby, and when he had accomplished that, then the English Derby—but this dream, for the fulfilment of which he relied much more on his trainer's indomitable efforts than on his own, only engrossed his energies in a partial manner, and left him time enough on his hands to feel that the world was occasionally wearisome. He would have liked to possess a large estate had that been practicable; but it was not according to his notions. If he were to begin forming a vast domain, it must be split up at his death and allotted in equal portions to his heirs, whoever they might be: and if there were half-a-dozen of these heirs, the portion of each would be about the size of an English yeoman's farm. This was beggarly. Had aliens been permitted to hold land in England, he would have got out of his difficulties by emigrating there and founding an estate under the tutelary auspices of primogeniture. As it was, he had more than once turned over the project of getting himself naturalized, only it was the probationary residence under some roof, not his own, which balked him.

Very correct in his attire, cut by an English tailor, shaved *à l'Anglaise* — that is, sporting moustache and whiskers, but no beard, and irreproachably gloved, he had adopted the habit of driving down to the Rue Ste. Geneviève in his phaeton to see Horace. But somehow he generally came at hours when his friend was absent : and this furnished a pretext for stepping into the shop below and staying sometimes half-an hour, sometimes more. The visit of a prince might be a rather appalling circumstance in the life of a British haberdasher : especially if that prince had a prancing equipage and a groom in livery waiting for him at the street corner; but the shoulders of Frenchmen are equal to any weight of honour. After the first interview or two, M. Pochemolle set down the frequent calls to the pleasure M. d'Arcola probably took in his, M. Pochemolle's, conversation. There would be nothing strange in that. M. le Prince and he held, he had observed, identical views on most points. When talking politics, M. Pochemolle said: " We men of order " — implying the solidarity existing between all persons of conservative mind—such as the Prince and himself—as against the disorderly or *canaille*.

That Georgette was not so blind need hardly be said. As she plied her needle in seeming unconsciousness, the motives of the Prince of Arcola's frequent visits could not quite escape her. At first they importuned her, these visits, and she scarcely opened her lips. But women who have been slighted are wounded in their self-love as well as in their deeper affections, and there was nothing unnatural in the fact that a homage which raised her in her own eyes by proving that all men were not as disdainful of her as Horace had been, should come to be regarded, not with pleasure indeed, but with something approaching to a mild sense of gratitude. She now and then hazarded a timid answer to some of the Prince's remarks, and her mother said she was beginning to look better.

"I am not more fortunate than usual," said the

Prince, walking into the shop with a smile, after inquiring uselessly for Horace one afternoon, some five weeks after M. Macrobe's fête. "Madame Pochemolle and Mademoiselle, your servant. M. Pochemolle, why this is seditious literature: are you, too, on our friend's committee?"

"Why, no, mon prince; I was just reading one of the addresses M. Gerold has circulated," responded M. Pochemolle, ruefully, and he displayed an enormous yellow poster, headed: "*Dixième Circonscription Electorale de la Seine. Candidature de l'Opposition. Circulaire à MM. les Electeurs.*"

"I hear the candidature is progressing remarkably well," said the Prince, accepting the seat which the draper hastened to offer him. "M. Gerold has a capital list of names on his committee, all the Orleanist phalanx, Baron Margauld at the head of them."

"And yourself, M. le Prince?" asked Mdme. Pochemolle.

"No, I am not on it, being no free agent; from father to son we must be Bornapartists in our family. But I give good wishes, and anonymous subscriptions."

"Which is what M. Macrobe does too, I hear," said M. Pochemolle, sighing. "Dear me, M. le Prince, this is a most awkward predicament; I never voted for a Republican in my life, except when they were in power, yet I could never bring myself to vote against M. Gerold."

"Providence has left a door of escape out of every human dilemma, M. Pochemolle. A cold in the head or an attack of gout are never-failing excuses. M. Macrobe, too, was in a difficulty. As Chairman of the Crédit Parisien, and newly-appointed Knight of the Legion, he could not decently have taken open part against the Government. So he labours under the rose, and is most indefatigable. If Gerold gets through it will be mainly owing to him."

"He is a most honest man, M. Macrobe, and the shares of the Crédit Parisien continue to rise every day," said M. Pochemolle.

"I shall be glad to see M. Horace deputy," remarked his wife; "though there will be no reading his speeches in the paper now that the Government prohibits parliamentary reports. He will have a silver-laced uniform, with a sword, and twelve thousand francs a year."

"Supposing he be elected," added the Prince, doubtfully, "but I am afraid it is not so sure. You see how the Radicals are treating him: they have refused to support his candidature; and that new paper of theirs, *Le Tocsin*, assaults him in a most scoundrelly way."

"Yes, I brought a copy of it home yesterday," grinned M. Alcibiade Pochemolle, who was measuring enough calico to make a petticoat. "They blackguarded him like good 'uns—said he only wanted to get into the House to finger the salary and then turn his coat and betray the party. I never read anything like it. M. Horace killed that other journalist for much less than that."

"Why should not the *Tocsin* say all this if it be true?" said Georgette calmly, without raising her eyes from her work. "It is a newspaper's duty to enlighten the public."

This was the first time Georgette had spoken, and her remark was so unexpected, so utterly at variance with the habitual gentleness of her speech, that everybody remained silent-struck. The Prince, who was seated close to the counter behind which she worked, examined her rapidly, and noticed that her lips were set, that her eyes gleamed, and that her needle-hand, as it stitched with feverish haste, trembled, and often missed the point. She looked up and repeated quietly : " M. Horace Gerold has given no proof that he is better than other men. It seems to me that gold is the only thing for which people care nowadays. For that they would sell their bodies and their souls."

" Georgette ! " exclaimed M. Pochemolle, scandalized and frightened ; and Mdme. Pochemolle, letting fall her work on the floor, grew red and white by turns.

The Prince, divining some emotion which had found its vent in the impulse of a wild moment, and which doubtless was already repenting having betrayed itself, came quickly to Georgette's relief.

"Mademoiselle speaks in a general way," he said. "She means that electors are so often imposed upon that they may be excused for being a little suspicious. I agree with her, and think that under existing circumstances we may perhaps make special allowances for our Radical friends. They have not a single representative in the House, and they are naturally anxious to get a member who will reflect their peculiar views better than M. Gerold, who, as Mademoiselle says, is as fond as we all are of the comforts and refinements which money procures."

Georgette thanked him by a glance. M. Pochemolle drew a sigh of satisfaction, having swallowed the explanation with entire faith. Mdme. Pochemolle, whether her woman's acuteness accepted it or not, pretended to do so; and thus the Prince was enabled to divert the conversation into a new channel. He had brought tickets for a new play which was making everybody weep at the Théâtre de la Gaieté. If there was one thing Mdme. Pochemolle liked more than another it was to have a good evening's cry over a melodrama, particularly when this satisfaction was afforded her in a stage box presented by some generous donor.

"And you will go, too, Mademoiselle, if you allow me to counsel you," said the Prince, speaking not very loud.

Though she had not yet recovered from the quiverings of her nervous excitement, she answered with more attention than she had ever lent him before: "What is the play about, Monsieur?"

"It treats of a young girl," said he slowly, and looking at her, "who has been faithlessly abandoned by a man she loved . . . ."

"Yes," continued she, interrupting him whilst her eye flashed, "abandoned for a woman who had gold to give. Go on, Monsieur, the story is an old one."

"Another man — of a different character — touched by her condition, pitying, admiring and loving her, offers her his heart . . . ."

"And she?"

"Accepts . . . ."

"I think not, Monsieur le Prince," returned she calmly. "The girl answered that she stood in no need of pity ; that admiration is not always a tribute to be proud of; and that for a man to offer his heart to a girl who is not his equal is but another way of saying that he thinks her fallen lower than she is."

CHAPTER XI.

CANVASSING.

GEORGETTE's outburst of wrath and abrupt revulsion of feeling as regards Horace were not mere caprice. They were due to her knowledge of what had passed between him and Angélique. In her dismay at the unforeseen climax brought about by her negotiations in favour of her friend, Angélique had at first known neither what to say nor what to do. She had taken four weeks meditating over the matter. Then the conviction had gathered within her that it would be honest to tell Georgette the whole truth: and she had done this, concealing no detail, but setting down everything as it had happened with the entire conscientiousness and want of tact which distinguishes those "who mean well."

From this confession Georgette had had no difficulty in gleaning that if Angélique did not actually love Horace herself, yet his declaration had so far unsettled her that she would have no strength to resist him if he prosecuted his courtship with anything like insistance. The fact is, Angélique's first essay at diplomatizing had completely exhausted all her powers of initiative. She had laboriously collected all her weak forces for an attack, and had been not only repulsed, but placed suddenly in the position of assailed. She could do no more. If M. Gerold was in earnest in what he said, if he had really set his mind upon marrying her, if, above all, he had her father for an ally, as she somehow suspected he would have, there would be no use in her offering any opposition.

Georgette saw this, and her mild spirit was roused. She would have forgiven Horace for not loving her, and had he married any brilliant woman of his own rank, rich or poor, from love or ambition, she would have excused him and borne her wound with resignation. But that he should be aspiring to the hand of Angélique Macrobe revolted her. This match was too sordid. Angélique could have nothing in her but her money to attract such a man as he. She was devoid of sense, her father's reputation was tarnished, their wealth was sprung no one knew whence, and had been publicly denounced as corrupt by Horace himself less than a year before. She felt all her love shrink into scorn for a man who could prostitute himself to such a debasing alliance: the more so as she was humiliated that Angélique in her clumsy and unauthorized attempts to plead her cause, had probably degraded her in the estimation of this man whom she now blushed at having worshipped. It is to be remarked that the idea that Horace's affection might be owing to other causes than monetary ones, to Angélique's beauty, for instance, was the only one that escaped Georgette. But this is a venial foible. Women are as much at a loss to discover personal attractions in their rivals as men to perceive talent in their adversaries.

The Prince of Arcola drove home in that state

of mind which inevitably follows a "scene" in the case of those who are unused to those incidents. He dined at his club—an English habit which he was helping to acclimatize by his example—and, being alone, had leisure to wonder how much truth and how much comedy there was in Mdlle. Georgette's performance. What puzzled him was the part Horace Gerold had played in all this. He should have been glad to know more of Gerold, who appeared to him a sort of social enigma — a man credited with enormous wealth, and living in the Rue Ste. Geneviève; a Republican whose austere principles were cited, and who danced at fancy dress-balls; a strictly virtuous youth who ravaged the hearts of draper's daughters. Then whom did Georgette mean by the woman to whom Gerold had sold himself for gold? He thought there would be no harm in trying to elucidate some of these points next time he met Horace. He could ask him frankly whether there had really ever been anything between him and Georgette, and how far matters had gone.

In the evening, at a party in the Faubourg St.

Germain, he stopped Jean Kerjou, the journalist, who was passing in all the glory of swallow-tails and crush-hat.

"It's a while since I have seen you, M. Kerjou. Can you give me any news of Gerold? He is, of course, very busy?"

"You know, mon prince, he is on our paper now—on the *Gazette des Boulevards*. Yes, he is up to his neck in election work, and we are toiling by his side. He will have the Orleanist votes, and the Legitimists are not disinclined to support him. Indeed, it is rather for the object of canvassing that I am here this evening."

"Then his worst enemies are the Reds. What can they mean by mauling him so pitilessly?"

"Heigh, it is their nature; but what makes the thing rather hard to stand is that amongst them are some men Gerold knows and used to be friends with. The Radical candidate who opposes him is that fellow Albi, and one of the writers of that rascally *Tocsin* is no other than Max Delormay whom Gerold defended in the libel action. He is not a bad character, but has a soft head—in fact, he is a fool—and I expect Albi corrupted him in prison. Then the *Sentinelle* has not behaved over well. Gerold counted that it would fight for him, but Nestor Roche has answered somewhat drily that his principles oblige him to remain neutral: which, under present circumstances, is as good as being hostile."

"Then what do you think?"

"We shall win, I hope; but it will be a tough struggle."

Yes, it bade fair to be that, and an exciting struggle as well. For the first time since the *coup-d'-état* a Parisian constituency was to have the opportunity of expressing its opinion with regard to the diversely-appreciated régime Frenchmen were undergoing since 1851. Bonapartists argued that now was the time to prove one's gratitude for the Crimean War, the victories of Alma and Inkermann, the International Exhibition of 1855, the cessation of street riots, the wholesale demolition of old houses, and the unexampled prosperity of trade. The Opposition retorted that here was the moment for asking where France's liberties were gone, what was done with the millions of increased taxes imposed upon the country every year; and, finally, what was the equivalent in dignity, peace, and happiness which the country was deriving from the suppression of its Republic? Paris was the only locality in the whole empire where the elections could be conducted with any independence; and the tactics recommended by the more acute amongst the leaders of the Opposition were formidable. If adopted, the Government could stand no chance against them. They consisted in this:—To bring forward as many candidates of various shades of opposition as was possible on the first day of polling, and to bind them by this common agreement:—That the one who obtained most votes on that *first* day should be left to stand alone against the official candidate on the *second*, all his brother opposition candidates retiring in his favour — *i.e.* requesting their electors to vote for him.*

---

* To illustrate this system of tactics, which led to the total defeat of the Government in the Paris elections of 1863, we will

As soon as it had been published that the seat of the Tenth Circumscription was vacant, a fair array of Oppositionists had entered the lists: a Legitimist count, who had not the ghost of a prospect; an ex-deputy of Louis Philippe's time, who had sat behind M. Thiers, and might be supposed to rally the bourgeois votes; a second ex-deputy, former supporter of M. Guizot; and finally Horace, who, at the cautious solicitation of M. Macrobe, announced himself simply as "Liberal," and whose candidature excited that interest which generally attends youth, courage, and a promptly-won reputation.

<small>take this example:—A constituency contains 35,000 electors. There are 5 candidates in the field, 1 Official and 4 Opposition, the latter comprising 1 Legitimist, 1 Orleanist, 1 Moderate Republican, and 1 Radical. On the first day of polling the 35,000 votes are distributed as follows: Official Candidate, 15,000; Moderate Republican, 8,000; Orleanist, 6,000; Legitimist, 4,000; Radical, 2,000. No one having secured the absolute majority, —*i.e.*, the half of the votes *plus* one (17,501)—a second day's poll becomes necessary; but this time, in accordance with their previous agreement, three out of the four Oppositionists retire in favour of the foremost amongst them; and the result is that the Official Candidate, who, on the first day, headed the poll by 7,000 votes, finds himself completely swamped on the second, the numbers being, Republican C., 20,000; Official C., 15,000. The Imperial Government so much dreaded this strategy that the project of abolishing the system of *ballotage* (second day's poll) was more than once seriously mooted.</small>

Everything was progressing favourably. That numerous section of Liberals who did not care who was elected provided it were an opponent of the Government, were looking sanguine, and the candidates had already entered into negotiations with a view to forming the desired coalition, when the sudden entry of the Radical candidate on the scene, and his loudly-expressed intention of co-operating with nobody not endorsing his own creed, had completely changed the face of matters. M. Albi, or the Citizen Albi as he called himself, was too popular with the working-class element for the coalition to offer any probability of success without him. The policy to be followed now was not to scatter the Opposition votes amongst the five or six candidates, but to put forward one man whose popularity might outbalance both that of Albi himself and the influence brought to bear in favour of the official nominee. Horace's original competitors were modest enough to perceive that their own popularities were not equal to this double emergency. They admitted that their only chance of entering the House was through the reciprocal system, and therefore they had retired at once, leaving the honour of fighting the unequal battle to Horace.

Everything that could be accomplished by a powerful committee disposing of considerable funds was now done to effect the return of young Gerold, who, bitterly stung by the animosity of his former allies, had plunged into the struggle with a determination to spare nothing to win. He was the man on whom, for the moment, the eyes of all Paris—nay, of all France—were fixed. People were hoping in him by hundreds of thousands—perhaps by millions. Journalists he had never known, whom he was never likely to know, were advocating his cause day after day in terms which made the blood thrill in his veins, and sometimes brought tears to his eyes. He had all the independent journals, both of capital and provinces, behind him. Certes, it was a fine position for a young man who had done nothing. But this very unanimity only made it the more exasperating that the paper he would have most liked to possess on his side—the honest and esteemed *Sentinelle*—had refused to speak a word for him.

"I should not be acting comformably to what I deem my duty as a Republican, were I to recommend you as deputy," had said Nestor Roche, coldly in answer to Horace's request. "The most I can do is to remain neutral."

"May I know what is your ideal of a Republican candidate?" Horace replied, speaking with suppressed wrath.

"I doubt whether you would be able to realize such an ideal, even in thought," responded Roche, grimly. "It is not that you dislike Republicanism, but you love other things more."

And Horace had been unable to elicit anything besides this.

As for Albi and Max Delormay, he had made no efforts to ascertain the motives of their enmity. Albi he had never liked, and Max Delormay was a personage who, ever since his imprisonment, had been haunted but by one thought—how to turn his political martyrdom to a good account. Now that he was out of prison, his joining a paper where he was twice as well paid as he had been on the *Sentinelle*, was a perfectly natural incident; nor was there anything very astonishing in his battering suddenly, for wages' sake, at an old friend: journalists are used to these brotherly demonstrations. What did surprise Horace, though, and many others with him, was that Albi, Delormay, and the rest of the set should have found the funds needful to start a paper; and still more, that the Government, which stringently prohibited new journals of moderate liberalism, should have licensed such a red-dyed, spit-fire organ as the *Tocsin*. This last circumstance, taken in conjunction with the relentless, furious war which the Radicals were waging against him, forced him to the conclusion that Government looked upon these men as its surest auxiliaries, and his detestation of their ignoble scurrility became tempered with something very like contempt for, what he was generous enough to consider, their blindness.

Police regulations allowed of no public meetings in which a candidate might address his electors, neither was a personal canvass in a constituency numbering rather more than fifty thousand voters a very practicable expedient. Official candidates got over these difficulties by convoking meetings within covered buildings, such as a theatre or concert-room, stuffing those who came with cake and wine, and then blandly declaring that this was nothing more than a private party; but the success of this stratagem would have been doubtful in the case of liberals. Their only means of making themselves known was to scatter circulars profusely, to go the full length which the Press laws allowed in the matter of newspaper-puffing, and to visit the workshops where a good many hands were employed and there make brief speeches, if so be that the foremen allowed it.

Horace's committee, of which M. Macrobe appeared to be the life and soul, though he only figured on it anonymously, had undertaken the distribution of the circulars; it disseminated them by cartloads, and not in the Tenth Circumscription alone, but throughout all Paris. It had, moreover, set an army of agents afoot, and a legion of bill-stickers, and a squadron of trusty pedlars who went about the Boulevards hawking cigarette-papers, lucifer-matches, and stationery, in boxes labelled GEROLD, and were often dragged off into custody for their pains. The newspapers launched leader upon leader, paragraph upon paragraph, and printed in flaming capitals on the top of their first columns:

"VOTE FOR GEROLD — CANDIDATE OF THE LIBERAL AND DEMOCRATIC OPPOSITION."

Some published letters from eminent politicians proscribed by the Empire, letters dated from exile and wishing god-speed to their young successor. Amongst these was one from Manuel Gerold. In a private letter to Horace he had pointed out with emotion and pride how great and unprecedented was the honour which the liberal party of Paris were conferring upon a man so young; in his public letter he recommended his son to the suffrages of the electors in the name of those past services for which he himself was suffering banishment, and vouched for Horace's Republicanism and fidelity as for his own. The visits to the workshops were performed by Horace of an afternoon and evening —he gave all his leisure time to them.

Emile accompanied him in these expeditions, and generally Jean Kerjou or some brother writer. The electioneering stirred all Emile's energies into activity. Nothing short of such an event as this could have drawn him away from his books and his briefs, but to further his brother's candidature, he abandoned both book and brief, gave himself up with all his steady power of application to the object before him, and was worth any dozen agents put together. Workmen are always delicate electors to handle. French workmen especially require to be managed with peculiar art, and Emile possessed that art; which, after all, was nothing but sterling sincerity. Where Horace failed to touch the sympathies of his hearers from speaking too much like a fine gentleman, and in language evidently coined for the occasion, Emile arrested their attention at once, and in a few pregnant sentences went to their hearts. They recognized in him a man who felt what they felt; his look,

his voice, his gesture, all told it them. More
than one sullen brow relaxed under the homely
magic of his words, more than one stubborn foe
was shaken, and there were days when murmurs
of assent broke out, worth twenty salvoes of
applause. Still, the canvassing in the popular
workshops was woefully up-hill work. The candidature
of Albi, and the denunciations of the
Tocsin, made havoc of Horace's cause amongst
the more excitable spirits; and the neutrality of
the *Sentinelle*, favourite organ of the artisan
quarters, damaged him sorely with the intelligent
workmen.

In this manner, five or six weeks flew by, until
the day when the writ was issued. This formality
precedes the election by three weeks, and in the
interval the zeal of both sides redoubles—it is
like the final period of training before the day of
the race. Bets were being offered on this election,
and the odds were in favour of Horace; for people,
as usual, judged by the superior noise which his
candidature was making. Emile received congratulations,
and predictions of success; but he

shook his head rather apprehensively: "I wish peace could be made with the Albians," he said; "we have a common foe, and when the enemy is so strong, disunion bodes little good."

This idea preyed upon him, and he had already turned over to small purpose an assortment of plans likely to operate a reconciliation, when one evening, not a week before polling-day, Horace decided upon canvassing a large workshop where some hundred men were employed in cabinet-maker's work. That day, as it happened, the *Tocsin* had been more than usually vituperative, and honest Jean Kerjou was indignant.

"By Heaven," he exclaimed, as he walked between the two brothers, "I don't know what withholds you from strangling these curs with your hands. It will be all I shall be able to do to keep my stick off Delormay when I meet him."

Horace said nothing.

"It is infamous, certainly," remarked Emile; "but we had better not strangle anybody. Disdain is as effective, if union be completely out of the question."

"You say 'if,'" cried Jean Kerjou. "Your brother has the patience of Saint Onesiphorus, who received a box on the ear, and begged the donor's pardon for standing in the way. Horace, you don't mean to say you could hold any terms with these vermin? I'd coalesce with the Government against them, and if any of those who voted for them on the first day offered to vote for me on the second, I'd throw their dirty suffrages back into their faces and ask them what the devil they take me for."

They reached the workshop. It stood in a not very savoury alley, and was preceded by a dingy court-yard, usually resounding with echoes of wood-planing, grinding of saws, and clanging of hammers. This time it seemed as though the workmen must be absent, for the place was silent, but as they advanced they caught the sounds of an impassioned voice raised as if addressing an assembly; and as all three climbed a dingy staircase, with a greasy wall on the one side and a shaky baluster on the other, a tremendous shock of applause burst like a thunderclap over their heads and a hundred pair of boots pounded the floor with a din that made the building tremble.

"What's this I wonder," exclaimed Jean Kerjou—they were pausing outside the door. "'Pon my word I believe we've actually stumbled on the badgers."

Horace pushed the door and they entered. Jean Kerjou's guess was right.

On a joiner's table, encumbered with tools, and shoved hurriedly next the wall at the end of the room in guise of platform, stood Albi, his hair dishevelled, his quick, wild eyes glancing fire, and his parched body drawn up in the attitude of one who is taking a moment's breath after a telling oratorical hit. Max Delormay, who had allowed his beard to grow, and was trying, without much success, to look as if he burned with hatred for tyrants, sat below him, glowering under a wide-awake; and the body of the hall was filled up with workmen in paper-caps and shirt-sleeves, leaning against or sitting upon unfinished articles of furniture, chests of drawers, cupboards and bedsteads. The floor was littered with wood-shavings and glue-pots; broad planks of oak, maple, and rosewood met the gaze; a clean smell of saw-dust and French polish pervaded the atmosphere.

All eyes were fixed upon the new comers, and a dead silence supervened. Who were they? Albi and Delormay alone winced and changed colour slightly. Horace lifted his hat and introduced himself in a few words, amidst a long murmur of curiosity. He concluded by saying: "As you are being addressed by one of my competitors, gentlemen, I will wait and claim the favour of speaking to you in my turn when he has finished."

"But this did not suit Albi, who, feeling no desire to have Horace and Jean Kerjou at arms'-length of him whilst he proceeded with the rest of his oration, yelled out at the moment they were moving towards the platform: "This is no place for aristocrats and sycophants."

There was a sensation.

"No," roared he, following up his advantage. "Keep out those men, citizens, who come with smooth words to ensnare your confidence. The poor have suffered enough, I should think, from having put faith in men who betrayed them. If

France is bowed down in chains and tears at this minute it is from having trusted in adventurers. Back! Tell them to go back to their masked balls, their operas—anywhere they please out of the sight of honest workmen whom they and their compeers have reduced to slavery. See! they have nothing to offer you but lying promises, and they quail miserably before your looks. Citizens! what the Workman wants is his lost liberties, his independence, the sovereignty that was ravished from him four years ago when he was off his guard—these men will bring you flatteries; your liberties and your sovereignty they would not give you if they could . . . ."

An ominous murmur rose. It is doubtful whether many there present cared much for their sovereignty, or were even conscious that they had lost it; but Albi spoke with a communicative fervour, his hand was stretched out menacingly, and the three strangers, instead of cowering under his harangue, seemed, on the contrary, both contemptuous and arrogant. Emile, it is true, sought to utter some words of quiet protest; but the Legitimist Jean Kerjou thwarted this endeavour by shouting with fury, "You rascally hound, if all your party were of the same mud as yourself, the ravishing of your liberties was the wisest thing that was ever done, for slavery and dog-whips are the only things you are fit for."

At this there was an immense clamour. "Knock him down!" cried a young workman, with solid arms. "Chuck them out!" chorussed twenty voices more. "Stand back!" roared Horace to an individual who was flourishing a rule over his head, and as the individual only answered with a grin, a crashing blow, levelled straight between the eyes, sent him backwards into the wood-shavings. The rest of the scene was enacted amidst clouds of dust, scuffling, blasphemies, heavy *thuds* of bodies rolled over on to the floor, and finally the opening wide of a door, and the precipitate descent of three persons down the staircase, with a tempest of valedictory howls from behind.

The candidate and his two companions found

themselves in the yard, bruised, dusty, torn, but not bloodstained, and minus their hats.

Jean Kerjou felt in his pockets, and discovered that his watch and purse were intact.

"It must have been an oversight of theirs," he remarked quietly.

CHAPTER XII.

VOX POPULI.

At last the day of election dawned—a glorious day of lustrous sunshine—the weather for great events or popular solemnities. Horace awoke with confidence, though pale and full of resentment, for the treatment he had endured in the workshop was rankling in his memory, causing him profound humiliation, mingled with a now burning desire to crush his rivals. The Radicals had attempted to make political capital out of the event, and the *Tocsin* had published a fantastic account of how the " pseudo-liberal " candidate had been expelled with ignominy " by the outraged artisans whom he had sought to cajole." This had led to the instant despatching of two seconds with a demand for a formal retractation, which had been accorded; Max Delormay opportunely remembering the fate of Paul de Cosaque. But neither the fantastic account nor the retractation had done Horace much good. His friends opined that he would have done well to let the attack pass unnoticed, and the *Tocsin* uttered piercing shrieks at what it called this violation of the liberty of the press by one who termed himself a Republican.

"This weather augurs favourably," said Emile, looking out of the window as the neighbouring belfry of Ste. Geneviève chimed nine o'clock.

"Yes, the shopkeepers will not stay at home as they do when it rains," added Jean Kerjou, who had come early. "I have seen more than one French election marred by showers which kept the rain-fearing classes within doors and allowed the tag-rag and bobtail to have it all their own way."

A knock, and M. Pochemolle entered in his Sunday coat and hat, clean-shaved and most respectable. After much mental tribulation and long doubts as to the course he ought to pursue, he had arrived at the conclusion that as the two votes of himself and his son could not possibly affect the general result in a constituency of fifty thousand, he would generously give them to M. Gerold. So he was now come to say that he and M. Alcibiade,—who, by the way, exercised his civic privilege for the first time—had risen betimes in order to record their suffrages as soon as ever the doors of the Mairie were opened. "And we were certainly the first who voted, Monsieur," added he, with effusion. "Ay, we were alone in the room with the Mayor and the gendarmes," chimed in M. Alcibiade, whose hair was profusely oiled for the occasion. "What they call the 'urn' is a long box with a slit in it, and when I saw that, I thought I might manage to slip in several voting tickets together— I'd got my pocket full of them—but the mayor didn't allow us to put them in ourselves. It's he who does it."

Another knock, and in sailed M. Filoselle with a new waistcoat of more striking tartan pattern than any before witnessed, and lavender gloves to match. He bowed with ease. He too had been voting, having come up to Paris for the special purpose the night before. " Yesterday morning I was at Marseilles, M. le Marquis, and deep in a negotiation for sending a cargo of cracked bugles to China, where they could pass for new, the Chinese not being musical; but I said, ' Duty before profit,' and here I am. When that sun sets may you be deputy for Paris, then I shall return to Marseilles as pleased as if all the cracked bugles in Christendom had been shipped to Pekin, and I had received seven per cent. on the commission."

This cheerful commencement to the day removed the cloud from Horace's brow. He dressed himself with care and sallied out with the intention of paying a visit to the Hôtel Macrobe, professedly to see its owner, really in the hope of meeting Angélique. His interviews with the financier's daughter had not been many since the scene at the fancy fête. Whether it was that she avoided him, or that he was unlucky in his hours for calling, she never seemed to be alone when he was in her company. There was always the Marquis of This or the Count of That, and sometimes bevies of ladies engaged in solving grave problems affecting the shape of a bonnet or the length of a skirt. If he could have outstayed these nobles and these ladies—but then M. Macrobe remained or Aunt Dorothée, which was proper and correct but embarrassing, insomuch as when she was not actually obliged to take part in the conversation, Angélique sat, resplendent and divine, but silent.

On the election morning, however, M. Macrobe pretexted having a letter to write before going out with Horace to the committee-room. He withdrew; Aunt Dorothée was upstairs, and Horace found himself for a moment alone with Angélique. It was in the boudoir which the financier had fitted up with such luxury and taste for his daughter. Rare objects of art gleamed on tables and consoles, choice flowers reared their scented heads out of exquisitely-tinted vases. Angélique's beauty shone with greater radiance amidst these surroundings, like a peerless jewel out of a costly setting. She was dressed in white and wore a single rose in her hair. A glancing sunbeam fell upon a curl that rested on her shoulder and made it glisten like spun gold.

As the door closed behind her father she blushed and rose, feigning to examine a scarlet jardenia. Horace approached her with emotion.

"Will you let me offer you a flower?" she said, as if to ward off words which she expected yet shrank from, and she broke off the finest sprig. But, as soon, she clasped her hands, blushed deeper, and said, "But no, I am forgetting that this is the day of your election and I am offering you the colours of your adversaries —those bad men who, they tell me, say such cruel things.

"And does it pain you that bad men should say such cruel things? But give me the flower, it has a price now that you have culled it."

He took it from her hand and fixed it in his button-hole. She continued to gaze at the jardenias but found nothing more to say; so he gently drew her hand in his and murmured: "Do you know why this day is so anxious a one in my life? It is because it may prove the starting-point to a career of honour which I shall lay as my only fortune at the feet of her I adore—at your feet."

She turned to him with blushing and almost piteous entreaty.

"Oh, why do you say that to me, M. Gerold, when Georgette is so much better and worthier of you than I—you, who are a famous man, who will become a great one, require a partner who is clever and can aid you. I could not do that—I know I could not—and I should make you unhappy, however much I tried to do otherwise."

"I do not want a partner who would aid me by cleverness," answered Horace, softly. "There is a help more potent than that to brace the nerve and smooth the path of man, and that help you could give if you tried to love me a little. Promise me that and you will make me more than happy."

Her bosom heaved, and in her trouble she could only falter:

"If it were really for your happiness, M. Gerold;

but it is not. Oh, I feel it is not! But, tell me, did you never, never love Georgette?"

This question, which revealed the first timid germs of feminine sentiment, transported him. He pressed her hand to his lips: "Never," he said, decidedly; "never."

Footsteps resounded outside. Instinctively they drew apart.

"Now then, my dear young friend, I am at your service," said M. Macrobe, returning. "My child, make your best curtsey to M. Gerold, who, before you see him again, will be the most enviable man in France."

Elections in France under the Imperial system were not the noisy and boisterous events they are in certain other countries. Although this election was regarded with mortal anxiety by a full million of French Liberals, who watched in it for the first feeble symptoms of independent revival, the streets showed little or no signs that anything unusual was taking place. It was a Sunday, as French polling days always are, the church bells rang, citizens, with glossy hats on their heads and smart wives on their arms, were trooping to the Bois de Boulogne or to the railway stations to catch excursion trains; and there was the customary sprinkling of soldiers in dress uniforms, some of whom, to be sure, stopped and stared a moment at the yellow, red, and white candidate's addresses glaring on the dead walls. But this was all. It was only in the quarters comprised in the 10th Circumscription that any electoral movements could be witnessed, and even here the proceedings were of the simplest character. The Circumscription was divided into twelve sections, and in each one of these was a polling place provided by the Municipality—that is, a room hired on the ground-floor of some eligible house decorated for the occasion by a tricolour flag. Anybody was free to enter these rooms on condition of standing quiet. They contained two gendarmes, a deal box with a slit in the lid, a table, and behind the table a half-dozen gentlemen, delegates of the Mairie and of the different candidates, seated on chairs. The electors came up one by one, handed their voting tickets folded to the municipal officer, who dropped them at once through the slit, and then retired in silence. No shouting, no cheers, no party cries. Outside some touters distributed voting papers to new-comers, and knots of two or three electors loitered in the roadway discussing the prospects of the candidate they favoured. But these groups were never allowed to congregate into crowds. A couple of *sergents-de-ville* paced watchfully up and down, saying, " Circulez, messieurs, s'il vous plait, circulez."

Horace's committee-room was in a street not very far from the Rue Ste. Geneviève. When he drove up to the door with the financier he found the nearest approach to a throng that he had yet seen that day, and a good many hats were lifted as he alighted—one or two hands even pressed forward to shake his. Inside, the room was crowded with Horace's friends and with newspaper reporters come to pick up the latest news. The *Gazette des Boulevards* mustered in great force, so did Mr. Drydust, who had brought a youthful British peer with him, the Viscount Margate, and was describing to his lordship the mechanism of universal suffrage both amongst that and other peoples. A shout arose as Horace darkened the doorway, and fifty voices were raised to announce to him the results of the first four hours' polling, as gathered approximately from the ticket-distributors at the different sections:

   Gerold 2,300
   Bourbatruelle 1,200
   Albi 450

There might not be much in these figures, for a large number of electors came with their voting tickets in their pockets and did not accept those proffered at the doors; still, they sent a flush to the face of the triumphing candidate. Mr. Drydust declared aloud that they must be taken as conclusive, the numerous elections he had seen having invariably been decided by the results of the first four hours' polling.

M. Bourbatruelle was the official candidate. It was not very easy to elect a personage suited to this delicate post in a city such as Paris, and under the circumstances, M. Bourbatruelle was really not a bad choice. He was a manufacturer of clay pipes. Every clay pipe in Paris issued from his stores bore the name of *Bourbatruelle* printed in small letters next the mouthpiece. On bringing him forward, the Government had suggested that it would do no harm to print this name of BOURBATRUELLE a little bigger, to prefix the words VOTE FOR, and to disseminate a hundred thousand clay pipes, thus amended, gratis amongst the population. M. Bourbatruelle had improved upon the hint by causing screws of shag to be bestowed along with the pipes— which was not bribery, although it might have been deemed so had M. Bourbatruelle been a Liberal, but simply a small token of affectionate generosity. There was a general impression current that M. Bourbatruelle was a fool—an erroneous idea, for a man is not a fool who can make himself a millionaire by selling clay-pipes. If the Corps Législatif were ever called upon to pass a law affecting the pipe-industry, everything tended to show that M. Bourbatruelle would prove himself thoroughly competent to defend his interests. Of course, as regards laws that had no connection with pipes, M. Bourbatruelle was indifferent, and was expected to be so, for had it been otherwise he would not have been chosen for official candidate.

M. Bourbatruelle had behaved like a gentleman towards Horace, leaving a card upon him and bowing to him with great civility once when they had met in the street. Horace had followed suit in the matter of the card, and returned the bow with respect. He had no animosity for M. Bourbatruelle, and it gave him keen pleasure to see that he was completely distancing Albi.

"I see every hope of our obtaining the victory, M. Gerold," said the grave and emphatic Baron Margauld. "Madame de Margauld has charged me to convey to you her good wishes. I think she has been not unoccupied in canvassing for you among some of her friends."

"I am most grateful," answered Horace, earnestly, "and whatever be the result of the election, believe me I shall never forget the kindness that has been so freely lavished on me."

Jean Kerjou ran in breathless.

"I have just come from the section of the Rue de Tournon. Emile came there to vote, and brought ninety-two workmen with him—all rabid supporters of Albi. He had talked them over. Ah, you should have heard him! You've got a brother there who is not made of ordinary stuff. If he had time to go the round of all the workshops by himself to-day, you would fly to the top of the poll like a flag to the masthead."

The voting begins at eight in the morning and concludes at six, and it is from this latter hour that the real excitement of a Parisian election commences. But the centre of animation is not so much in the voting quarters as on the Boulevards. On those three hundred yards of holy ground between the Opéra Comique and the Théâtre des Variétés every man flocks who holds a pen or a pencil, who may wear a gown or an epaulette, who is anybody or anything—journalists, artists, barristers, officers, novelists, stockbrokers, all jumbled together, smoking, chattering, gesticulating, and waiting for the evening papers. At half-past six on the evening of the election you could not have dropped so much as a pea from the balcony of one of the houses of the Boulevard Montmartre without its alighting on the hat of somebody. The crowd surged rather than flowed. The cafés were crammed to suffocation—not a seat to be had in them.

The lamp-lighters, with their long ladders, found themselves unable to make any head against the current, and appealed distractedly to be allowed to pass. In the kiosks, the newspaper-women, worn out with counting money and folding broadsheets, had hung out the announcement which is their signal of distress: "No change given." And amidst all the din, the clinking of glasses in the cafés, the rattling of dominoes on the marble tables, the cries of "*Oui, Monsieur; tout de suite,*" from the waiters, snapped the exclamations, "Gerold wins!" "I'll lay on Albi: they say the Radicals polled in the afternoon." "I vote an address of condolence to Bourbatruelle."

Of a sudden, a tremendous rush. A string of news-boys were coming full tilt down the Rue Montmartre, metropolis of printers, with the second edition of the *Gazette des Boulevards*. They are mobbed. The kiosks are stormed. A deluge of copper coin ensues—those who have no sous give francs, and the papers are torn open :—

"Latest News.

"*At the moment of going to press with our second edition the results of the election are still uncertain; but the contest has been a very severe one. Until two o'clock the Liberal candidate maintained the head; but the majority of electors did not poll till late, and it is now supposed that the votes are so equally divided that a 'ballotage' will be necessary. The greatest order prevails.*"

Ten minutes later the second edition of the *Sentinelle* appeared, and was cleared away in two minutes :—

"Election of the 10th Circumscription.

"*The votes are being counted as fast as possible in the different sections, and it is now beyond doubt that the Government have sustained an overwhelming defeat, the aggregate of votes given to the two opposition candidates amounting to almost double the number polled by the official candidate. M. Horace Gerold's committee are sanguine; but at M. Albi's head-quarters it is confidently asserted that the immense majority of votes polled in the afternoon were for the radical interest. We have no means of ascertaining how far this rumour is correct."*

Finally, at about eight, an impossible, indescribable scrimmage greeted the third edition of the *Tocsin*, brought damp from the press by men wild with excitement, and shrieking: "*Final Result!*"

This is what the *Tocsin* printed:—

"CLOSE OF THE POLL.
TRIUMPH OF THE RADICAL CANDIDATE.

10th *Circumscription.*

Number of Registered Electors . . 51,515
Number of Votes recorded. . . . 45,963
Absolute Majority required. . . . 22,982

ALBI 19,310
BOURBATRUELLE. . . 14,518
GEROLD 12,125

None of the candidates having obtained the absolute majority, a 'bailotage' will take place this day fortnight."

This news was brought to Horace in his committee-room, and he managed to glide out unperceived amid the consternation and tumult which it occasioned. He had not eaten since the morning, excitement having left him no appetite, and he now felt faint; his steps were hurried and unsteady. People passed him with contented faces, returning home after their Sunday walk; and how he envied those people, who probably led uneventful lives and had no ambition! In a quiet street an Italian was grinding an organ and a ring of little children danced around him filling the evening air with their gay, crowing laughter. He rather wondered that these children did not read on his face how disappointed and unhappy he was, and pause in their merrymaking; but he tried to smile to them kindly, and he thought the music the sweetest, most pathetic he had ever heard. When close to his lodgings, he stopped, remembering Emile. His brother would take this to heart more than he himself would. He must go in looking unconcerned, cheerful, if he could; he rehearsed one or two things which he could say to console Emile. And so he reached the Rue Ste. Geneviève.

But just as he was about to cross the road opposite M. Pochemolle's house, he was arrested by a loud and jubilant clamour proceeding from the end of the street and a joyous crowd debouched uttering shouts of triumph and escorting a man perched high aloft on a pair of stalwart shoulders. It was Albi's constituents chairing him from his committee-room to his home. The police had made some sort of effort to prevent it, but they were too few, and the men too many—something like a couple of hundred; besides which, the procession was only noisy, not obstreperous, so that it was best to let it alone. On they came, cheering with all the power of their lungs, and tossing their caps into the air; and the inhabitants, attracted by this sight of by-gone times, came out on to their doorsteps, to look and nod, and clap their hands: success excites applause, like sunshine the song of birds. Horace remained standing where he was, motionless; but just as the exulting troop approached, a window facing him was opened, and Georgette appeared. She looked out and saw him at once. He was standing in the full light of a gas-lamp—she at an angle where her features were plainly visible—and their eyes met. Rapid as lightning she darted on him a look of contempt and derisive triumph, and at the moment when the vanquishers swept beneath her, leaned forward, caught up a nosegay that was standing on the sill, and threw it to Albi.

CHAPTER XIII.

MACROBE À LA RESCOUSSE!

To have been during three months the most prominent man in one's country, to have dreamed of becoming, at an age when others are subalterns, the unique representative and leader of a party that numbered the best, wisest, and greatest men of France—and to find oneself suddenly fallen again to the position of writer on a second-rate newspaper, was bitter enough. But what redoubled the chagrin and mortification of Horace was the way in which his supporters of yesterday —the journals that had been his champions— hastened to desert him and passed to the side of his rival. So long as it had been a question of choosing between two candidates—one an educated gentleman, the son of an illustrious patriot, and a proved Liberal like Horace; the other, a darksome and not over well-known revolutionist like Albi—the moderate, enlightened organs of public opinion had not hesitated. But now that the ultimative lay between taking the official candidate or having Albi, the issue was changed. After all Albi was a Liberal, he would not vote as the other two hundred and sixty members in that servile, voiceless chamber. He would raise his cry on behalf of proscribed freedom; he would protest against the laws of tyranny passed in the name of France. It was absolutely necessary that the Opposition should have, at least, one spokesman; and the liberal journals unanimously called upon Horace Gerold to retire in Albi's favour. To make matters worse, Emile, though he did not verbally urge this course, implied by his manner that he desired its adoption; and Manuel Gerold, writing from Brussels, spoke of it as imperative—as a thing that did not even admit of discussion. "The life of a public man," he wrote, "must be one of self-sacrifice. Personal ambition, predilections, rancours, must all sink before considerations of public good. This man was your enemy yesterday, to-day you must be his ally; else your electors would have the right to think it is yourself you wished to serve, not them."

To resign in favour of Albi, to further the return of a man who had pursued him with uncalled-for spite, marred his own certain triumph, and who, had the positions been reversed, would never have given way to *him*—having vowed not to do so when he started—this was an act of magnanimity which demanded superhuman courage. Horace blenched at it; it chilled his heart to think of. Nor did his judgment incline to it readily; for was not this man a malicious, serpent-tongued slanderer—had he not shown himself both tortuous-minded and unscrupulous, and was it to be supposed that the Liberal party could be benefited by having such a personage as that for its representative? In his perplexity he sought the Hôtel Macrobe, as much to cheer himself after his cruel deception by a look at and a word from Angélique, as to ask counsel of the financier whom he was beginning to look at as his mentor. But, as though all creation were conspiring against him, neither Angélique nor her father were at home. So he walked back sorrowfully and betook himself to the society of his friends of the *Gazette des Boulevards*, the only paper which had remained faithful to him, and whose advice, as conveyed energetically by Jean Kerjou, was "not to abet the entry of a blackguard into Parliament."

M. Macrobe was not at home, because closeted in private conversation with M. le Ministre Gribaud. This time the financier was subjected to no ante-room delay as at his last audience. On his arrival the venerable Bernard had saluted him to the ground, and ushered him at once into the Minister's presence, and M. Gribaud had motioned to him with his finger to take a seat.

"Well, M. Macrobe," began his Excellency, rather sourly. "It seems we've overdone it."

"I certainly thought the official candidate would get through, your Excellency. It never entered my thoughts that this man Albi could make such a hit."

"Nineteen thousand votes, and twelve thousand given to young Gerold: thirty-one thousand Oppositionists in one constituency! Ah! how right we are to keep the curb well strained: how quickly this devil-city would overturn us if we let it! But now what is to be done? Albi of course will not retire; but will Gerold do so in favour of our man, as you predicted?"

"Things have not turned out as I had planned," answered M. Macrobe, with his brows knit. "I had counted that the two rival candidatures would divide the Opposition votes and allow the Government nominee to get in easily; but then I had not foreseen that the Opposition was so strong. As for Albi, we have no hold on him. He came forward on the understanding that his expenses should be paid and that he should have the funds to start a paper. It was necessary to find a name which would rally a certain number of Radicals; but I imagined that he would get ten thousand votes at the most and that when he had served our purpose we could simply let him drop and suppress his journal. But, for the present, it would not be safe to try this. He does not know that it is the Government who have brought him forward; he fancies it is a Radical Committee, and if this committee were to play him false at such a moment, just as he was on the point of succeeding, he would suspect something and denounce it aloud; for though he be a vicious, venomous brute, he is no traitor. No, he must never learn that the committee under whose orders he has been acting is composed of men in the pay of the Prefecture, and that all his contributors on the *Tocsin*, with the exception of that simpleton Delormay, draw their inspirations from Ministerial source. The scandal would become public and injure the Government. What we must do is to defeat Albi on Sunday week; then the committee can say that, his election having failed, they see no use in continuing the paper, and withdraw their caution money. But first we must beat the man, and now there remains but one way to do that; only one."

"Which? If young Gerold will retire in favour of Bourbatruelle we might manage. There cannot be much love lost between him and the *Tocsin* I should think." And his Excellency chuckled a little.

"No, there is not. He hates Albi ten times more than he ever hated the Government, and if left alone would throw the Radicals overboard without much parley. But he is influenced by his brother—a young prig—and by his father, so that although I should not actually despair of bringing him to coalesce with us, yet the thing would require an effort and more diplomacy than it would be worth. I say more than it would be worth, because it is not so sure that even if Gerold did resign in Bourbatruelle's favour, all his electors would obey him. The unexpected lead taken by Albi has roused the hopes of the Opposition. All their papers are now backing Albi, and supposing that out of Gerold's twelve thousand electors, eight thousand were to vote for the official candidate, and four thousand only for the other man, Albi would still win. I suggest, your Excellency, that the man who should withdraw is M. Bourbatruelle. His supporters would naturally poll for Gerold whether they were asked to do it or not, and these fourteen thousand votes would beat the Radicals out of the field."

"And Gerold; how will he behave when he is in the House? You were not encouraging on this score last time we talked the matter over."

"True, your Excellency; but the conditions are altered. If Gerold had been elected as an Opposition candidate, he would have given us trouble, but if he gets in now, he will readily perceive that he owes it to the Conservatives. The affair, however, must be managed with tact. Let Monsieur Bourbatruelle withdraw without recommending his electors to vote for anybody. The majority of the Opposition press, deeming that Albi, with his nineteen thousand original votes, has the best chance, will probably continue to support him; the Government press, on the contrary, will take up Gerold's colours, and this will serve to widen the breach which the first day's poll has made between the Liberal candidate and the Radicals. Once in the House, the conviction that he is virtually representing a constituency of Bonapartists and temperate Liberals will keep Gerold within bounds. He is not likely to forget the party that opposed him so ruthlessly, and he will feel proportionate gratitude for the men who secured his triumph. A little courtesy and tolerance on the part of his colleagues will do the rest. But if the worst comes to the worst—I mean, if Gerold proves unmanageable—he need not remain in the House more than a year. We are in 1856; in another twelvemonth come the general elections."

His Excellency M. Gribaud rubbed his left ear thoughtfully, then cracked the joints of his tough fingers.

"Well, we will try your plan," he said, slowly. "It's rather like admitting a young wolf-cub into a sheep-fold to put this Gerold into the Corps Législatif; but perhaps the cub's teeth are a bit blunted. I will send for Bourbatruelle at once. We shall have to give him something. H'm, the Legion of Honour will do. Then we shall have to pay his expenses. By-the-way, Gerold has not got a *centime*, of course ; and I suppose you've not found out what he and his father do with their money ? I learn from the sub-prefect at Hautbourg that charitable donations are sent by them every quarter-day ; but the town complains that it is ruined, root and branch."

"Better days will perhaps come for it," answered M. Macrobe, laconically.

"Yes, if you succeed in your *rôle* of General Monk."

"Who is General Monk, your Excellency ? " asked M. Macrobe, for, though an astute financier, his historical education had been neglected.

"General Monk was a shrewd fellow who restored a penniless young king to his estates and then helped him to govern them," said M. Gribaud, grinning broadly.

A slight tinge of colour came to M. Macrobe's parchment countenance, but he laughed.

"Well, I hope he was well repaid, your Excellency."

"Oh, yes, it was a good speculation, as you gentlemen of the Bourse say." And, continuing to grin, M. Gribaud took up his pen and indicted a line to M. Bourbatruelle, the clay pipe manufacturer. "This will do the business," he said; "but mind, Monsieur Macrobe, I am acting now in deference to your judgment, and we shall regard you in some way as surety for this young fellow's good behaviour."

The financier made an obeisance, and, the audience being now terminated, withdrew.

But he did not go straight off to Horace to hold out the plank of safety which he had just hewn out for him. Events had marched fast, but the time had come for accelerating them, if possible. Horace Gerold had entered the net, the meshes must now be closed upon him rapidly; he must be brought to propose for Angélique, to break with his party, and to place himself in M. Macrobe's dependence, all at one swoop. This could be effected by leaving him to his misery for these next few days. He must be left to drink to the dregs the cup of his humiliation—to chafe and writhe under his abandonment; and then, when all the world seemed bitterness and deception to him, his future father-in-law could step in like a *deus ex machinâ*, smoothe away his troubles, and send him careering once more on the high-road to glory. So M. Macrobe merely wrote a line to request Horace not to take any step as to retiring until the following Sunday—seven days before the second ballot—when his committee would consider the subject, and by the same post he arranged that M. Bourbatruelle's retirement should also be held in suspense until the same date. This done he sent Mdlle. Angélique into the country with her aunt for a day or two, and took an easy opportunity of having Horace informed by a third person that this young lady was being wooed by the Prince of Arcola, and would probably soon be asked in marriage by that nobleman. "If he really loves her," argued M. Macrobe, "this will make him miserable and furious; if it be a mere inclination, jealousy will stimulate it, and, no doubt, fan it into something warmer."

Thus the week passed by. The posters with Albi's name were renewed on the walls; the *Tocsin* gloated over its victory and reviled the conquered; the chorus of journals which besought the liberal candidate to do his " duty " swelled every day, and Horace himself was as thoroughly galled, distracted, and despondent, as can be imagined.

On the Sunday he paced his room in an agony of doubt, trying to form a resolution, yet not daring to take it.

" I don't see that there's anything to hesitate about," grumbled royalist Jean Kerjou, who was imbedded in an arm-chair and puffed solemnly at a cigar. " The moral sense of this generation seems to be blunted. What ! Here is a cur whom you would not admit into your back kitchen, and half the newspapers of France are laying their heads together to plan how they may foist him upon an assembly of gentlemen ! God bless the days when there were no parliamentary institutions to make such tricks look excusable in the name of party tactics. Heaven bless the times when there existed a free-masonry between gentlemen to send rogues to Coventry, and when fellows like Albi were shunned like the pest."

"It's not the man we should be helping into the Corps Législatif, but his principles," answered Horace feebly.

"Oh, his principles, my dear M. Gerold," exclaimed Arsène Gousset, laughing. He had come with a dainty-looking volume of somewhat improper poems—his composition —which were being much read in fashionable spheres, and which he desired the *Gazette des Boulevards* to handle tenderly. "What principles do you think those men have, except this immortal one, to turn out every man that holds a place and to put themselves in his stead? You will say he is a Republican, but so is every man who has not a *centime* and sees no chance of ever possessing one; and this is no more a title of honour than to say that his trousers are ragged, his washerwoman's bill unpaid, and that he dines off boiled beef, not being able to afford venison. The rich and educated who join this band are either perspicuous citizens who want to climb the political ladder quickly, and know that there is no better stepping-stone for their purpose than the heads of the unwashed; or amiable enthusiasts, like your father, who would govern wolves with kind words and jackals with forms of logic. As soon as these excellent theorists get into power, they begin by locking up the dog-whips, chains, and collars; they proclaim the liberty of howling; and a few weeks after they are howled out of office—as your father was. The fact is, the doctrine of Republicanism starts from the assumption that, however ignorant and brute-like an individual member of the lower orders may be—and that he *is* both ignorant and brute-like is sufficiently proved by our interminable schemes for educating and refining him—yet, that a few millions of such individuals, putting their ignorance and brutishness in common, become a class full of sense and virtue, both worthy and competent to rule; which seems to me like contending that, although one of the jackals above-mentioned, lean and ravenous, might be a danger to the poultry-yard, yet that a good big troop of such jackals turned loose together among the hen-coops would show the world what abstemiousness was, and extend a brotherly protection to the fowls. I should like to get a Republican candidly to acknowledge—but they never will do so—that Republicanism, as we understand it nowadays, has never existed anywhere, and when tried has eternally broken down. Greece and Rome were aristocratical oligarchies, in which all the lower orders were slaves. It was much the same thing at Venice, Genoa, and in Holland : republican in name, virtually close vestries, in which no man was admitted to power who had not a square cash-box to recommend him. In South America, democratic Republicanism—considerably diluted, however, by the slavery of the negroes, who do all the servile work—has been on its trial nearly half a century, and has resulted in a revolution every twelvemonth. There have been in Chili since the independence something like twenty *coups-d'état*, in Peru rather more ; in Mexico the people change their executive as they do their shirts. As for the

United States—where again we find the negroes, who represent the proletarian classes of Europe, kept under heel — Republicanism has hobbled along hitherto there because, the country not being half peopled, there is land, like air and water, for all comers; and the subversive gentlemen, who in Europe swarm in our large cities and overturn our governments for us, go out into the West and found states of their own, where liberty, equality, and fraternity flourish under the shade of the bowie-knife, the revolver, and the bludgeon. But in a hundred years hence, when the descendants of these squatters begin to wash their hands and fence in their properties, when there is not a rag more land to distribute to immigrants, and when it becomes a question of providing for several million paupers, I doubt whether apostles of the Albi school will be more appreciated in American upper circles than they are with us. State prisons and gibbet-trees will be erected on their behalf, as they have been in this land; persecutions, revolutions, and reactions will succeed one another like a rotation of crops, and the States will pass through their cycle of monarchies even as the rest of the world has done. You see, there are certain orders of things you will never be able to reconcile, and amongst these is the Empty Stomach and the Full One. To the end of time, the man who has not dined will be the foe of the man who has, and the history of revolutions is but that of the alternate triumphs of these two over one another. To-day it is Gribaud and Company who dine, to-morrow it may be Albi and Brothers. Only, to think that Albi Brothers have any object but to get this dinner, or that, if they once had the keys of the state larder, anybody save themselves would be the better for it, is one of those bright fallacies that denote a cheerful contempt for the lessons of history. Revolutions never abolish abuses—they only change them. We have gone through three bloody revolutions, and four changes of dynasty, to set over us M. Gribaud, who presses as heavily on mankind as ever did the Duc de Choiseul or the Marquis de Maurepas; a fourth revolution would give us M. Albi. Upon my word, I consider things are very well as they are; the change would be insignificant in so far as results went, and it would cost money, to say nothing of comfort."

The Court Novelist emitted all this in his most lively tone of bantering persiflage, blowing wreathing clouds of smoke towards heaven, and stroking his carefully trimmed yellow beard with a hand on which glittered an enormous diamond, the gift of an empress. But his paradoxes did not offer any solution to Horace, and when, at length, he smilingly withdrew along with obdurate Jean Kerjou, whose parting words were to "fight till grim death, as my Breton countrymen do," Horace began striding up and down as before, but more harassed, vacillating, and moody than ever.

"Duty!" he exclaimed, bitterly, "what do men ever gain by performing it?" and he thought of Georgette and her unfeeling insult on the evening of his defeat. It was an insult the more cruel as he was unable to divine the motive of it. He had been wrong in flirting with Georgette; he had felt this, and retreated before it was too late both for himself and for her. But was this the way to be revenged on him? When he met her by chance, she glared upon him with the eyes of a little tigress, or, what was worse, treated him with undisguised, aggressive scorn, as if he were some abject criminal. She was not even content to trust to fortuitous occasions for making him feel her spite. One evening, returning home, he had found the work-box which he had given her lying on the table, and not a word of explanation with it, not a line to mark what she was offended at, or what he might do to soothe her resentment away. She was behaving without any sense or reserve. Had she been a misguided girl quarrelling with her paramour, she could not have acted otherwise; for, after all, he had given her no direct cause for offence. His sins, if sins they were, had been of a negative kind. He had left off seeing her because he wished to conduct himself as an honest man; and when, after a long interval, he had ventured upon entering the shop again, he had found the Prince of Arcola there. And this had recurred several times: more than once when he had passed the shop latterly, he had seen either the Prince himself or his well-known phaeton waiting at the corner of the street.

At this recollection of the Prince of Arcola his brow grew black.

M. Macrobe had not misreckoned on the emotion which the report of Angélique's marriage would cause him. The news had gone into Horace's heart like a knife. Coming at such a moment, when the cup of his mortification was already brimming, it was a savage sort of blow. It put him roughly back in his place, showing him what a poor devil he definitely was, and how extravagant was the pretension for one such as he to espouse a millionaire's daughter. Till that moment he had never reflected on Isidore Macrobe's wealth in connection with Angélique; but he did so now, and measured at a glance the distance that separated him—him, a struggling journalist and barrister—from the brilliant Prince of Arcola. So this Prince was destined to thwart him in his love, as that man Albi was doing in his ambition! At the outset of his career, he was to be stopped dead short by a dandified sportsman and a ranting demagogue; nay, more, he was asked in the name of duty to connive in this result! Angry and pale, he swore this should never be. He had torn himself away from Georgette, that she might be respectably married and never know trouble; and what was the consequence? She despised him for his pains, and coquetted with a Prince whose intentions towards her were clearly what those of most other men of easy morals would be in such a contingency. Now, people were soliciting him to make a new sacrifice, in order, no doubt, that Albi might laugh at him in his turn and take him for a credulous simpleton. No, no; as Jean Kerjou said, this was a case for fighting till the end. He would tell the Prince that a libertine, titled though he were, was no fit husband for Angélique; and if the Prince resisted, why there were means of settling these questions, in France, without much loss of time or words. As for Albi, committees or newspapers, friends or foes, might say what they pleased—if he could prevent that fellow from succeeding, he would do so; and if he could not, it should, at least, not be said, that it had been for want of the trying.

Whether by accident or design M. Gousset had wrapped his pretty volume of improper poems in a number of the *Tocsin*, and there they lay both on the table together, the improper fashionable book, and the improper democratic gazette. Horace suddenly caught sight of the journal, and, full of his new resolution, snatched it up and ran his eye over the leading article; as usual, an attack on himself, written by Albi, not without talent, but in a style of violence positively reeking with hatred and injustice. It was one of those infamous articles which are intended to stab deep, and which do stab, however steeled we may be against them by usage. Horace flushed all over as he read it. He crushed the sheet in his hand, and darting to his desk, penned a letter to the chief of the independent journals who were calling on him to retire.

He was so intent upon his work, his pen flew so rapidly over his paper, that he remained unconscious of the presence of M. Macrobe, who having knocked without eliciting an answer, had opened the door and glided in. When he had dashed off his signature, he looked up, gleaming.

The financier's eye was mutely interrogative. Horace handed him the letter without speaking.

M. Macrobe perused it with a nod.

"So far so good," he said, "this will do as a beginning; but men like you must do more than talk, they must conquer. You would not be sorry to crush this Albi?"

Horace's eyes glistened, and he waved his hand —an eloquent gesture—it meant, "Give me the chance."

"Then the day is yours," said M. Macrobe. "I have come to tell you that M. Bourbatruelle retires; you will remain face to face with Albi; but as you will have the votes of all the honest people who, thank heaven! are a majority, your return is assured."

Horace rose to his feet; it seemed to him in that moment that the room swam.

"Yes," pursued the financier calmly; "I saw M. Gribaud, and he said, "The Government prefer being criticized by a man of honour like M. Gerold, rather than by a low-bred person like M. Albi. Besides, all the votes given to M. Bourbatruelle belong of right to M. Gerold, for the electors of the Tenth Circumscription are liberal to a man, and if some of them vote for the official candidate, it is only out of dread for theories which are neither liberalism nor republicanism, nor anything else but blasphemy and blunder. If these electors had not suspected M. Gerold of making common cause with the revolutionists they would have elected him the other day." This is what M. Gribaud said. "He is much maligned, I assure you, is M. Gribaud. He spoke of you in the highest terms, and affirmed that the Government were particularly touched by the strikingly honourable way in which you had carried on the contest."

A tumult of emotions welled up in Horace's breast, and broke upon his face in changes of colour rapid as a succession of waves.

"M. Macrobe," he faltered, springing forward, "I am sure it is to you I owe this—it is you who have been working to secure me this triumph."

"Pooh, pooh! my dear young friend, I have done my duty, that is all. You owe nothing to anybody save yourself."

"No, no. You say that because you are too generous to accept thanks. You are continually befriending me, who have done nothing to deserve it; and how I can ever repay these acts of kindness and devotion is more than I know or can imagine."

"Why talk of that? Believe me, I am more than repaid already by the pleasure of serving you," said the financier, smiling. "I have but one wish, M. Gerold, and that is to see you prosper."

"Then add one more to your benefits, and complete my happiness," cried Horace, impulsively. "M. Macrobe, let me speak on a subject that is nearest my heart, but which I might not perhaps have dared to mention, had it not been for this new proof of the interest you bear me. I have had the presumption to hope that we might some day be connected by a closer tie than that of mere friendship. Yes, though I have nothing to offer but an honest name, and can compete with none who have great rent-rolls to give, I love your daughter. Yesterday I heard a report that Mdlle. Angélique was already betrothed to the Prince of Arcola, and the news caused me inexpressible sadness. If you could only tell me that this was not true, and cheer me with the assurance that I shall not hope in vain—that when I have created myself a position, you will allow me to pay my addresses to your daughter—you would be fulfilling my fondest desire, and I should look back upon this day as the most fortunate in my life."

M. Macrobe's features very cleverly expressed the greatest surprise, and he became grave.

"I had never suspected this, M. Gerold," he said; "but I should be dissembling were I to conceal how much your communication flatters me. I am unaware that the Prince of Arcola has paid his addresses to my daughter. I think the report must be a false one; but, in any case, rent-roll is the last qualification I should consider in any one who aspired to become my child's husband. I was a poor man myself, and have not found that wealth adds much to one's happiness. Honesty, courage, and ability are the only riches I set store by. In a word, my dear young friend, there is no man I would sooner own as my son-in-law than yourself."

In England, a man would have grasped the speaker's hand; in France they manage these things differently. Horace flung his arms round M. Macrobe's neck, and kissed him on both cheeks.

If he could have known the pleasure which this embrace gave the worthy gentleman!

*　　　*　　　*　　　*

On the following Sunday, Horace Gerold was elected Deputy of the City of Paris; though it was a close shave, as cognoscenti remarked. The Radicals, encouraged by their first success, came up to the poll multiplied, united, and strong. The Bonapartists rallied round the "Liberal" candidate, and the result was :—

Number of votes recorded, 46,347.

GEROLD 23,258
ALBI 23,089

That is, a majority of ONE HUNDRED AND TWENTY-SEVEN VOTES!

A few weeks later, the *Gazette des Boulevards* announced to the world that a marriage had been arranged "between the newly-elected member for Paris, our ex-contributor, M. Horace Gerold (the Marquis of Clairefontaine), and Mdlle. Angélique Macrobe, daughter of the eminent chairman of the Crédit Parisien."

CHAPTER XIV.

EPISTOLARY.

So M. Macrobe had won the first game of his rubber. Won it promptly, cleverly, and completely. The second now began, and from the outset it looked as if he would win that too. Ten months after the Paris election the following three letters found their way through the post:—

From Emile Gerold, Paris, to Manuel Gerold, Brussels.

"Rue Ste. Geneviève, January 7, 1857.

"MY DEAR FATHER,—

" I HAVE just come in from pleading a rather dry case before a not very intelligent judge, and I find your good, welcome letter awaiting me. This weekly correspondence with you, that is the reading of your missives and the pleasure of replying to them, constitutes the gleam of sunshine in my somewhat lustreless life. Not, mind you, that I complain of this monotony, for I have failed to perceive that those whose existences are more variegated seem much the happier for it. But it is nevertheless a relief to turn now and then from my habitual studies— the poor devices by which men may best outwit one another — to the perusal of language so vivifying in tone, so humanely loving, so full of generous truth as yours. It is like escaping for a moment into a purer world.

"Yet, on the present occasion, are there not traces of unusual depression in certain passages of your letter; I mean those in which you speak of Horace? I have no wish to allude unnecessarily to the events of the last few months, which I can guess have pained you and which I will not conceal have to some extent disappointed me. But be assured that, in so far as the heart goes, my brother is unchanged. He is, perhaps, a little sore at your not having come to Paris for his marriage, and it may be that this feeling reveals itself, as you say, by a slight tone of pique in his letters; but I do not think we should be altogether surprised at this, for it only argues the great value he attaches to your approbation and his extreme sensitiveness lest any of his acts should be susceptible, in your eyes, of misinterpretation. On this last score, it is true, I might reassure him; for that his marriage was one of pure affection, unalloyed by any mercenary thought, neither you nor I certainly ever doubted. But it is not enough to tell him this. In his present temper of mind, he requires us to approve without reserve *all* his recent undertakings. Binding up, as it were, his marriage, his friendship with M. Macrobe, and his political course together, he resents any stricture upon one incident as a blame upon all three; and it wounds him to the quick to suspect that you or I can even remotely concur in any of the harsh criticisms which these different occurrences have evoked from his enemies.

"No doubt this morbidly nervous mood will

give way in time to feelings more in consonance with Horace's naturally genial disposition; but until it does, I for one—half of whose contentment in life would be gone were I estranged from my brother—I submit to the necessity of the case and tacitly acquiesce in everything. I wish our party had behaved with a little more fairness and tact to him. That they should have called upon him to retire after that unlucky first ballot was natural enough, but I do think it was wanting both in justice and generosity to support Albi against Horace once the other man had retired, and to reproach Horace when elected with being an official candidate. From a mere party point of view it seems to me that it would have been more politic of the Liberals to claim my brother's return as a victory. He would have served their cause then and faithfully; but their almost disdainful repudiation of him, contrasting as it does with the singular courtesy and kindness shown him by the other side, are producing the only fruits that could be expected under the circumstances. Horace complains that he has been ill-treated, and never refers to the subject without indignant bitterness. Nevertheless, from what I can gather of the debates in the Corps Législatif —scraps of which, you know, reach the public ear through drawing-room echoes—his is the only voice in that gloomy building ever raised in defence of liberty. He opposes Government bills, advocates reforms which in times like these might be called subversive; and, were he stimulated by contradiction, I suspect he would go greater lengths in liberalism than many of those who essayed to brand him as a Bonapartist would dare do. But nobody contradicts him; I hear on the contrary that he is applauded. The plan of his adversaries appears to be to enthral him by civility, and there could in truth be no surer way of touching one who is as open to kindly influences as he is quick to feel injustice. However, there is a boundary line dividing Horace's now wavering attitude from total secession, and when he has reached this line and sees the pit beyond he may recoil. Such is my hope, I might add—my prayer.

"Meanwhile, domestically speaking, Horace is I believe happy. He resides in his father-in-law's house, and every time I visit him there I find him looking bright and pleased with his lot. His wife is a gentle, loveable young person, shy and rather silent, but I think good. She submits to him in all things, and his chief preoccupation seems to be to make her happy. M. Macrobe, at whose table I have once or twice dined, rather to satisfy Horace than myself, is also—I must do him that justice—very zealous in catering for his son-in-law's felicity. He bustles about, forms projects, agrees with everything Horace suggests, and to me in particular he is most attentive. The family circle has lately been completed by the arrival of a Crimean hero just returned at the Peace. His name is Captain Clarimon; he was introduced to me as a kind of nephew of M. Macrobe's, and is, so far as I could judge, a pleasant fellow. Horace and he appear to have already struck up a fast friendship.

"I perceive I have covered so much paper that

I will close here. I repeat, my dear father, how much pleasure your letters always give me; but it continues to be to me a source of daily increasing sorrow that your voluntary exile should be thus perforce prolonged, and that we should be compelled to exchange our thoughts in writing instead of by word of mouth.

>   Cui dextræ jungere dextram
> Non datur, ac veras audire et reddere voces.

Why does not this Second Empire fall and open the gates of France anew to all the great and good men who are sharers in your proscription?

"With tenderest respect and sympathy,

"Your affectionate son,

"EMILE GEROLD."

"P.S.—I have forgotten to mention that I may soon be obliged to date my letters from elsewhere than here, owing to the retirement from business of M. Pochemolle and the consequently possible sale of this house. The news took me a little by surprise when the good man brought it up to me in person yesterday, enveloped in pompously deferential explanations that made the gist of the communication at first a little obscure. He said that 'my esteemed connection by alliance, Monsieur Macrobe,' had been the instrument of his attaining more rapidly to fortune than he ever would have done had he confined himself to the beaten tracks of commerce. He had, by Monsieur Macrobe's advice, invested money in the Crédit Parisien, buying shares at 500 which were now worth 1,500, and the result was that Madame Pochemolle was recommending him to retire and purchase a villa with a garden and a pond—Madame Pochemolle inclined, said he, for gold-fish in the pond—somewhere in the suburbs of Paris. I could see that it cost the excellent man a pang to relinquish the *Three Crowns* to a stranger, and that so far as he was concerned, the shop where his fathers traded and the modest gains which they earned, seemed preferable to all the suburban villas in the world, with or without gold-fish. But, neither Madame Pochemolle nor Monsieur Alcibiade being of the same opinion, the draper is out-voted and will be set to perform—will-he, nil-he—the comedy of '*Le Rentier malgré lui.*' There was almost a touch of pathos in the way he exclaimed, ' Our fathers made their earnings slowly, and prospered long; I have gone further in one year than they did in fifty; yet somehow it doesn't give me the pleasure I should have thought. I keep fancying that money which comes so quickly into the pockets of those who have done nothing to deserve it, must have come equally quick out of the pockets of those who didn't deserve to lose it.' I promised M. Pochemolle I would apprise you of his change of condition. His words were, 'Pray, sir, inform my most respected preserver, with my humble duty, that selling cloth or wearing it, I shall remain as much his obliged servant as heretofore.'

"Ever affectionately,

"E. G."

From M. Hector Filoselle, London, to Horace Gerold, Paris.

"Leissester Squarre, January 15, 1857.

"Monsieur le Marquis,—

"I DATE this letter from the banks of the Thames in the metropolis of the Queen Victoria, whither I have journeyed upon business, and the occasion I seize is that of the Sunday repose, which in this great country reminds me of the repose of model convict prisons. Great Heaven! figure to yourself a square as large as the Place Vendôme, and not one soul visible in it but a single policeman, who is melancholy; and around and about this policeman closed shops and cafés hermetically barricaded, as if they feared an invasion; for the English law decrees that man shall not be thirsty of a Sunday morning, and the publican who sells him drink is fined by the tribunal of Queen's Bench two sterlings. These laws astonish the stranger. Also, I have noticed that it is interdicted to play music on the Saturday, for yesterday I witnessed a milord chase from his door, with indignation, a grinder on the organ, who was presently pursued by a policeman, and, as they told me, conducted to prison, where he will be judged by the tribunal of Habeas Corpus. However, these are details with which I have not the heart greatly to occupy myself; being sad, even to the point that the business questions themselves lose their interest for me. Ah, Monsieur le Marquis, it was not merely a superficial affection I nourished for Mademoiselle Georgette. I had long meditated the project of making her happiness and mine, and on the day when you interposed, speaking the good word for me, I cried to myself, 'Ah, it will become a reality, that dream I cherish!' But fortune and other causes, amongst which I suspect the presence of a rival suitor, have coalesced themselves to defeat my ardent hopes and your benevolence. Already, at my last visit but one to Paris five months ago, shortly after your own marriage, Monsieur le Marquis, I noticed that the attitude of my future father-in-law, M. Pochemolle, had undergone a change towards me, and that the demeanour of my future mother-in-law—whom I have ever gratified with a moderate liking—was chilly, not to say freezingly distant. On my next visit these impressions were more than confirmed, and now I am in receipt of a letter from Monsieur Pochemolle, which leaves no longer a place for doubt. He states that he relinquishes the draper's trade to devote himself henceforth to a retired life, and he adds that, under these altered circumstances, perhaps I shall see the propriety of breaking off an engagement which has ceased to be so suitable as it once looked. Alas, the good man! I know very well that it is not he who would write in this way; but husbands are the slaves of their wives, notwithstanding the Code Napoleon, and Monsieur Pochemolle does but express the sentiments that have germed in the feminine but unelevated soul of Madame Pochemolle. You will excuse me for making you thus the confidant of my destroyed illusions, Monsieur le Marquis, but I wished to assure you that even in this moment of grief, when the faithlessness of woman is once more exemplified at my expense, I retain a recollection full of gratitude for the manner in which you deigned to befriend me. Life is a bale of mixed goods out of which one draws at the hazard, to-day stuffs of bright colour, to-morrow, mourning crape. I this time have lit upon the crape. Well, well, it was fated; but at least this consolation is given me, to feel that Mademoiselle Georgette is, like myself, the victim of destiny, not the willing accomplice of a plot for ruining my well-loved castle in the air. Ah! the usages of the world forbid my now seeking any communication with her who was my betrothed, and my own pride will not permit me ever again to cross the threshold of those who have closed to me their doors. Yet should ever the opportunity present itself, I will say to Mademoiselle Georgette —as I would respectfully pray you to say for me should the opportunity come first to you—that I bear no malice, but wish my rival well. This is for Mademoiselle Georgette's sake, against whom I could not bring myself to feel anger even if I would. As for her mother—but no, I will take a noble vengeance on that woman. I will apply myself with aching spirit but with renewed ardour to the pursuits of commerce, in order that when I, too, have become rich, she may open her eyes to the mistake she has made, and murmur, 'I should have done better to give her to Filoselle.'

"Begging to enclose a prospectus of current prices of the house of Verjus and Tonnelier, wine-merchants, of Paris, whose goods I will guarantee sound; also the description of a new kind of bagpipe, patented by Messrs. Doremi, for whose house I travel, and three of which I have recently sold to Milord Ardcheanochrochan, a Scotch peer of distinction, I have the honour to offer you, Monsieur le Marquis, the assurance of my deepest respect and gratitude,

"Hector Filoselle."

M. Prosper Macrobe to his Excellency M. Gribaud.

"Avenue des Champs Elysées, January 21, 1857.

"Monsieur le Ministre,—

"I acknowledge the receipt of the report from the sub-Prefect of Hautbourg, which your

Excellency obligingly forwarded to me yesterday. I laid it, as arranged, on a table where it was sure to meet my son-in-law's eye, and he read it after asking me how it came that such a document should have fallen into my possession. I explained that the sub-Prefect was an acquaintance of mine who had sent me a duplicate of the copy he intended despatching to the Government in the hope that I would intercede with the Clairefontaine family to do something for the perishing town. 'Which,' added I, 'I should not have ventured to do had you not accidentally stumbled upon that report which I had mislaid.' He made no answer; but, during the rest of the evening, he remained pensive, and I could see that those passages of the report in which the sub-Prefect contrasts the now pitiable plight of Hautbourg with its flourishing condition when the Castle of Clairefontaine was tenanted, had produced upon him all the effect which I expected. I need not add—for your Excellency has doubtless been in a position to notice this fact yourself—how surely the great kindness and forbearance of the Government are operating on my son-in-law. I might adduce testimony of this in citing the very words he used when your Excellency, in the name of the Ministry, accepted the slight amendment he moved to a recent Police Bill. He said that 'whatever might be his opinions as to the reigning dynasty, Napoleon III. had a merit not common to his predecessors, that of selecting able ministers.' I have the honour to remain, Monsieur le Ministre, your Excellency's most humble and obedient servant,

"Prosper Macrobe."

CHAPTER XV.

A SPEECH, A VOTE, AND A SURPRISE.

IT is two o'clock. Luncheon is just over, and a group of five persons are congregated in one of the most sunny morning rooms of the Hôtel Macrobe. The financier, with his brass-bound note-book in his hand, is jotting down the details of some pecuniary transaction in which he does not look as if he had been fleeced. Aunt Dorothée is counting, with an air of wobegone solitude, the patterns on the carpet, as if to divine what average sum in copper money each separate flower must have cost. Beside her on the blue satin sofa her niece unravels a skein of bright worsted which Captain Clarimon, the Crimean hero and her cousin, is holding with docility; and Horace, his back to the mantelpiece, interrupts the silence to read aloud occasional paragraphs out of the newspaper he is skimming.

A footman enters powdered and majestuous, the incarnate image of "eight hundred francs a year and perquisites." "Monsieur le Marquis's horse is at the door," he announces. Horace no longer objects to be called M. le Marquis. Soon after their marriage Angélique—no doubt paternally instructed—remarked that she liked the title Madame la Marquise better than that of Madame Gerold. It was said in the same tone she would have adopted to state her preference for burnt almonds over candied cherries; but from that day Horace had suffered himself to be marquisized without protest. He was not responsible, however, for the sudden and violent eruption of coronets which, after this little uxorial victory, burst upon every article of furniture or piece of plate on which it was possible to paint or engrave these symbols. Even his linen he now noticed had been secretly seized and branded.

At the announcement of the horse Angélique

laid down her worsted and ran obligingly to fetch her husband's hat and gloves. She was the same pretty, silent Angélique as of yore. A shade more of timidity in her manner; a fainter shade of gravity on her beautiful face, and that was all.

Captain Clarimon also rose, displaying, when on his legs, a handsome giant six feet high, with bold, military face, moustaches waxed at either end as sharp as spear-points, and hands that must have held a firm grip of the cavalry sabre when cutting down rebel proletaries in the *coup-d'état* affrays or Russians on the field of Inkermann. Crimean heroes being still the rage at that period, Captain Clarimon had been made welcome at thè Hôtel Macrobe, and, finding his quarters good, evinced no disposition to desert them.

"So you are off to your legislative duties, Marquis," said he, with more veneration than might have been expected from one who had learned by experience what a poor show an assembly of legislators makes against half a troop of horse.

"Yes," answered Horace, smiling to his wife,

and thanking her as he took his hat from her hands. "Yes, Captain, but I don't know what we are going to legislate upon to-day. I have not seen the notice-paper."

"I think it is a colonial question," said M. Macrobe, shutting up his note-book with a well-satisfied snap; "the political régime of Martinique and Guadeloupe."

"Dull countries," remarked the Captain, "and cursedly peppery—ahem, I beg pardon, ma belle cousine. I lived in garrison there."

"Amongst the poor negroes," observed Angélique.

"Ay, the poor negroes who used to be slaves," exclaimed Aunt Dorothée dismally, as if the servitude of the black races had been the cankerworm of her existence.

M. Macrobe on the sly launched a thunderbolt-glance in the direction of Aunt Dorothée, and coughed to drown her misplaced sympathy.

"The negroes—yes, those poor fellows who used to be so happy a few years ago, and who now, by all accounts, are in a miserable state of destitution," ejaculated he.

"That's exactly it," laughed the Captain. "The beggars were happy enough until a number of Deputies, half of whom had never seen a negro, and the other half of whom had never talked to one, laid their heads together to set them free. Up to that time Martinique and Guadeloupe had been flourishing. The negroes were well fed, well housed, and had no more work than was good for them. But crack! down comes the abolition, and what's the result? Your nigger left to himself won't work at any price. Planters are ruined, trade dries up by the roots, and our two colonies go to the dogs. That's what comes of making laws," added he, sapiently.

"My father was amongst those who agitated for abolition," remarked Horace, rather drily.

"Of course, and quite right too," returned the Captain, unabashed. "I am sure I should have voted for emancipating the poor devils; in fact, I'm for emancipating everybody, and letting them all do as they like. But if you'd been to Guadeloupe, I fancy you'd wish they had delayed the experiment until you were past visiting the place again. Why, I have ridden twenty miles along the coast and met not a living soul save three niggers, all stretched on their backs in the sun, and swearing it was too hot to work. Like oysters, 'pon my word."

"Well, as I know very little or nothing about the colonies, perhaps you wouldn't mind riding down to the House with me and enlightening me," said Horace, cheerful again. "One picks up useful waifs in conversation. I will order a second horse to be saddled."

The Captain good-naturedly acquiesced, and so did M. Macrobe, who seemed pleased with the arrangement. A second hack was soon brought round, and the Captain armed himself with a riding-whip.

"Au revoir, child," said Horace, kissing Angélique on the forehead. "What shall you do all the afternoon?"

"Long to see you return," she whispered, with a slight, sweet smile, which brought a ray of pleasure to his eyes, and to her features a little colour. "Then, I have my round of visits to make," added she, submitting to the second kiss with which he rewarded her pretty compliment.

The Captain also took his leave in cousinly style. Selecting by hazard, no doubt, a moment when Horace's back was turned, he said, "Au revoir, charmante cousine," and, bowing, lifted her hand to his lips.

As the gallant warrior was thus engaged, M. Macrobe's eye was fixed upon him with rather a curious expression.

The debate had already commenced when Horace settled into his seat in the House—if debate it can be called where every honourable gentleman was known to be of the same opinion, and would infallibly vote the same way when the hour of "division" arrived. The Corps Législatif, indeed, had not been created that it might make itself much heard or felt. Its function in the constitutional machinery was to spin as noiselessly as possible; to do its little piece of allotted work in the way prescribed, but just that and no more; above all to avoid clanking or in any way jarring upon the nerves of its imperial proprietor. The look of the session hall marked its altered destination from what the place had been in days passed by. Where was the tribune whence Royer-Collard had delivered his flashing orations; Manuel, Foy, and Benjamin Constant hurled their fire; and where Guizot had stood at bay, breasting the attacks of Berryer, Lamartine, and Thiers combined? Gone. Where were the strangers' galleries in which two generations of Frenchmen had trained themselves to love of parliamentary eloquence, to worship of freedom? Where the journalists' box, in which, turn by turn, had sat all the master penmen who had moulded the thoughts of young France—Courier, Carrel, Mignet, Vitel, Sacy, Girardin? Present, but closed. Where the benches on which at one time and in one array, had figured Victor Hugo and Beranger, Louis Blanc and Quinet, Montalembert and Lamennais, Arago and Cousin? Present again, but peopled by two hundred and sixty gentlemen of debonnair aspect and facile manners, with not an idea between them but plenty of small talk; gentlemen culled pretty much to right and left as we gather mushrooms, from half-ruined estates, from the purlieus of the Stock Exchange, from plethoric and, consequently, loyal Chambers of Commerce, from the semi-official press, from ministerial backstairs, last and least, from court. All of which gentlemen had been shoved into the Corps Législatif to do their duty, and did it—voting as they were bid, and roaring very conscientiously, "Hear, hear," when a minister spoke, to the tune of five hundred pounds a-year a-piece.

As a counterpoise to these two hundred and sixty human and self-acting voting instruments, Horace's seat, slightly isolated from the others, being a little to the left of the President's chair, was the only one which could, by any elasticity of expression short of downright abuse of language, be termed independent.

As Horace entered, an obese legislator was sawing the air with his right hand, proclaiming the reasons which would induce him to vote in favour of the bill—a gratuitous piece of good nature which seemed so entirely superfluous to his colleagues that they serenely busied themselves in different ways and didn't listen to him. A large proportion of honourable members were writing their private letters, a good number more sprawling with legs outstretched, hands deep in pockets, and countenances upverted with a beatific gaze at the skylight, were sleeping the sleep of the just. Four or five, whom you had fancied poring with absorbed interest over statistical blue-books, were palpitating over the incidents of a steeplechase at Chantilly, described in the usual graphic language by a reporter of *Le Sport;* and a pair who kept their backs turned to the rest of the world, and were pushing white bits of something composedly towards each other, looked suspiciously as if they were playing at dominoes.

Horace was soon surrounded in his seat—colleagues in squads came smirking up to kill time with a little quiet chat until the rising of the House. He was not unpopular, the Member for Paris. Deputies fat and lean, jovial and bilious, broke into smiles as he passed them. In the lobbies he reaped as many hat-salutes and shakes of the hand as he knew what to do with. The prevailing notion was that, although independent, which was certainly a point against him, he was not dangerous, and might be trusted.

A canine-visaged deputy, with a rasping voice and a nose like a fig, said pleasantly:

"Shall we have the satisfaction of hearing you to-day, Monsieur le Marquis? A debate in which I take some interest. Was a planter myself in the good times."

"In the time of slavery?"

"Precisely. I had five hundred slaves and devilish contented they were. Never cow-hided them except when they deserved it. Within three years of the abolition half of them were underground; floated themselves to the deuce on rivers of rum. Ah, the rascals."

"I do think it's so absurd to talk of niggers as human beings," giggled a young viscount with features livid from long vigils and hair in curl. "The Marquise de Vermeillon had a negro page she dressed in red, and an ape she put in blue—

confoundedly *rococo* she was, the Marquise. And I used to say to her, 'Marquise, if those two exchange clothes I shall be giving sugar-plums to Snowball—this was the nigger—and my card to Adonis—this was the ape. Hee, hee, hee.'"

Everybody laughed. This was very funny.

"I lost a million francs by the abolition," resumed the fig-nosed planter, in a voice like that of a nutmeg on a grater, "but the colony lost more. Chaps that didn't understand anything about the niggers' interests, nor about anybody else's, those that suppressed slavery. Why, isn't there slavery in all countries more or less? Look at our peasants who are taken by the Conscription at twenty, made to serve seven years, and risk being shot into the bargain. The niggers risked nothing, there wasn't a cleaner, happier lot going; why, it was like a prime concert to see 'em squat in a row and whistle in the sun. Then we used to marry 'em——"

"Yes," grinned the young viscount; "and I've heard of a nigger who was henpecked like fun, until one lucky day his wife was sold to one master and he to another. That's an advantage that wouldn't have been open to him if he'd been a free Frenchman. Once spliced with us whites its always spliced."

More merriment, interrupted this time, however, by the sudden close of the obese member's speech. At this the House woke up for a moment and burst cordially, and without a moment's hesitation, into unanimous cheering. The members who were writing their letters, those who slept with their countenances heavenwards, those who were palpitating over the prose of the sporting writer, and the pair who played dominoes, all looked up and shouted defiantly, "Hear, hear!" as if there were an invisible opposition making itself obstreperous on the benches of the Left and requiring to be put down. Then the President, a dapper statesman, ornamented with a red ribbon and star, consulted a list on his table, and called out to another deputy to rise and say something. It was very much indeed like a schoolmaster crying, "Boy Duval, stand up and construe."

Unfortunately for the regularity of the proceedings, the honourable gentleman appealed to was absent, having been taken ill in the morning; so was the next member on the list, who had been summoned away by telegraph at early dawn to bury a relative; and the third deputy whose name the President called was not yet arrived—whence an unexpected hitch. These debates, to tell the truth, were all mapped out beforehand, like the programmes of a musical entertainment. In order that a sceptic public might have no handle for murmuring that honourable members did small work for their 500*l.* per annum, M. Gribaud, the Minister, and his Excellency the President, provided between them that no bill should be sent up to the Crown without a decent amount of preliminary speechifying to season it withal. They recruited talkative members—those preferred who had the great art of saying nothing, and putting it into a good many words. It would be arranged that Monsieur A. should get up and talk from two till a quarter past, that Monsieur B. should follow him from the quarter to the half-hour, and that when Messieurs C.,

D., and E. had each had their twenty minutes' or half-hour's turn, according as they felt in condition, Monsieur Gribaud himself should rise— towards five or thereabouts—reduce all their arguments to powder, prevail upon them to withdraw their suggestions or amendments, which they were not likely to object to do, and get the bill voted by acclamation in time for everybody to be home and dressing for dinner at six. Now, when Messieurs C., D., and E., all failed to come up to time together, it was tantamount to what the unforeseen eclipse of the tenor, bass, and baritone at one of Monsieur Hertz's morning performances would have been. Some little consternation ensued. The honourable gentlemen who were writing their private letters nibbled the ends of their quills, the pair who played dominoes looked guiltily apprehensive lest they should be dragged out of their retirement and forced to speak whether they liked it or not; Monsieur Gribaud, who had been sitting with his arms folded and his head drooping on his chest, in apparent slumber—though of all men in the room he was certainly the most wide-awake, drew out his watch, but seeing it yet wanted two hours to six, put it back again and frowned. What was to be done? Propriety scarcely admitted of the Minister making a general appeal for somebody to devote himself, and it would not have concorded with the dignity of a legislative council for the President to exclaim, "I vow nobody shall go out of here until I get my three speeches." In this emergency all eyes sought Horace. What is the use of an Opposition member if he be not prepared to spout by the hour at half-a-minute's notice?

So, drawn by that magnetic attraction which brings orators to their legs, Horace, without well knowing what he did, rose, and an instantaneous sigh of relief went round. He had not in the least made up his mind as to what he should say, neither had he caught a dozen words of what the last speaker had uttered—moreover, he was not quite clear as to what the bill's scope was. These were disadvantages, but, being a Frenchman every inch, they did not appal him as they might have done the scion of a less glib-tongued race. Certes, there was a difference between the young man who had stammered the first phrases of his maiden speech before the judges of the Police Correctionnelle and the coolly confident deputy of the people. The confidence of twenty thousand voters must make a man self-trusting if anything will. Horace began by running his hands through his hair, which seems to be a physical necessity with most Parisian speakers, and then, without hesitation, started into retrospective survey of the history of the French colonial empire, which would be sure to be appropriate. He alluded to Duplex and Lally-Tollendal; compared Lapeyrousse with Cook, somewhat to the disparagement of the latter; grew lyrical over Montcalm and the fall of Quebec, and towered to patriotic heights when describing how "the fairest jewels of our colonial crown" had been reft away by the avidity of a nation now at peace with us. This brought him to the negroes and the question of compulsory and gratuitous instruction, which, like the Messrs. Somebody's pills, appears to be the panacea for all evils known and unknown. "The negroes were lazy and allowed our colonies to be ruined; why was that? Because they were not educated. If the negro were taught to read, and gratified with a free press to develop his liberal culture, not a doubt that he would take to work with an ardent zeal. Commerce would re-flourish under his efforts, and France would show herself in colonial prosperity, as in other things, to be the mistress of the world." This conclusion was hailed, as it deserved to be, with loud, long, and general applause, for the great merit of the speech was that, although nobody had understood it, it had occupied a good hour in delivery. All that now remained was for M. Gribaud to reply, which he did with adroitness, declaring he should not fail to remember the suggestion of his honourable friend, and that the question of negro instruction would for the future be foremost amongst those involving his most attentive consideration. Whereupon there was more cheering, enthusiastic and long continued; the question was put from the chair, and carried *nem. con.;* the pens, newspapers, blotting-books and dominoes were stowed away, and everybody went home to dinner, France being the richer by a bill, and the Corps Législatif the happier for three speeches. Such is civilization.

In the lobby, going out, Horace was joined by the Planter, who, raspingly and bluffly as ever, said, "Fine wor-rds, Monsieur le Marquis, and a good deal of body in 'em too, I don't doubt. Only, in practice, reading and writing don't any more change the nigger's nature than soap can whiten his skin. I've been to Jamaica and there seen model schools built a good many years ago by an Englishman named Guineaman——"

"Guineaman!" interrupted Horace, with a start, for he recalled the name of his uncle's wife, the woman whose slave-earned money had restored Clairefontaine, and set a lasting stigma of indignity on it.

"Yes, a slave-trader," returned the fig-nosed planter carelessly, "but, like all Englishmen, one who kept the Bible in his tail-coat pocket and called it his compass. When he walloped a nigger he took car-re to quote the chapter and verse that gave him authority, and I believe he wouldn't have exceeded forty stripes, save one, for any money."

"A hypocrite?"

"Wa'al, no, it's bred in the grain. Those English who are pr-ractical have discovered that they can do a good many more queer things by citing the Bible than we Fr-rench can do without it. But I didn't know this Monsieur Guineaman; he was dead and gone long befor-re my time. They used to talk about him at Jamaica, though, and show the schools he built when he'd made his fortune; for it was his theory that slavery being lawful—for the Government didn't for-rbid it then no more does the Bible now—he'd just as much right to tur-rn an honest penny that way as anybody else, provided, of course, he didn't bully his niggers, which I think good mor-rals. The-refor-re, as I say, he opened schools and preaching-houses to make the beggars lively, just as I at Martinique being Fr-rench, set up dancing booths to the same end. Only, my dancing booths tur-rned up tr-rumps and Monsieur Guineaman's schools didn't. The niggers danced jigs fast enough, but be hanged if they loved r-reading and writing any more than hoeing and digging. It's not in the nature of the varmin."

Which wise commentary brought the two legislators to the door of egress where both found their broughams. The fig-nosed planter wedged himself snugly into his and was whirled away to one of those banquets which kept his physiognomy in such perpetual glow; Horace was going to follow suit, and had already one foot on his brougham step, when a familiar equipage, drawn by two superb bays and driven with right British science, came like a hurricane down the Quai d'Orsay, ten yards off where he was standing, whirling up a spray of mud-drops and flint-sparks on its passage. The driver was the Prince of Arcola, who recognized him, and instantly reined in his steeds with consummate skill, clattering and champing on their haunches.

"This is a lucky meeting. I will give you a lift."

"With pleasure," said Horace, who was always

glad to see the Prince; and he scrambled into the phaeton, which, as soon as released by the two cockaded grooms who had sprung to the horses' head, sped merrily on its course again.

"I have been on a call to some old friends of yours," said the Prince, as they debouched into the Champs Elysées with a speed that made the gaslights flit past them like flakes of fire thrown up by an engine in motion.

"I have almost as many friends as enemies now, Prince," was the smiling answer.

"I mean the Pochemolles."

"I have not seen them for an age," said Horace, with interest. "I heard last month they were going to retire, but when I went to congratulate M. Pochemolle on his rise in the ladder, he had already removed. They are all well, I hope, and the good draper is not yet counter-sick?"

"They are installed at Meudon," rejoined the Prince without smiling. "The villa is a pretty one, devoid of vulgarity, the dwelling of an honest man who retires on a loyally-earned competence.

Both Monsieur and Madame Pochemolle are very well."

"And Georgette?" inquired Horace, after a moment's silence, though looking with something of archness at his interlocutor.

As if he had been expecting the question, the Prince quivered slightly. He did not immediately reply, but lashed his horses nervously into a faster trot. Then abruptly he turned his face full on Horace's and said: "Gerold, I have been wanting for the last twelve months to put you a question, but have never dared—you will guess why, perhaps, some day. Tell me now, on your word, between man and man, has there ever been anything between you and Georgette?"

Horace, though he had long suspected the Prince of paying a more or less avowable court to the draper's daughter, was little prepared for the attack, and changed colour.

"Nothing of any importance," said he, evasively, and rather trying to laugh off the subject.

"Then there *has* been something," muttered

the Prince, and it seemed to Horace that he turned pale.

"I swear to you that, so far as I know and believe, Georgette is a virtuous girl, if that is what you mean," he said.

The Prince seemed relieved; but musingly he exclaimed: "Then what is the significance of her flaming up as she does whenever your name is mentioned?"

Horace wondered. Why Georgette should thus flame up was to him inexplicable except under the hypothesis that she was an extremely forward person. He had not forgotten the whimsical display of spleen to which she had treated him a few months before, when the report of his marriage was beginning to gain ground: but this was a thing of the past now, which he was fain to dismiss from his mind as not worth brooding over. Besides, a woman's fair fame is a thing against which a man with the least spark of feeling is so loth to breathe a careless word, even when he has cause for suspicion and motives of personal rancour, that Horace checked himself on the point of making a rejoinder that would have reflected slightingly on Georgette's conduct towards him, and answered guardedly: "As her father's lodger, I frequently saw Mdlle. Georgette, and it may be that by occasional civilities, by those unmeaning compliments which we men pay without attaching any weight to them, I suffered my intentions to be misinterpreted. In this case the blame would be mine, not Mdlle. Georgette's, and she might feel some resentment at what may seem to her to have been levity on my part. This is the explanation I suggest."

"And that is all that passed between you— positively all?"

"That is all."

"Well, you have taken a load off me," murmured the Prince, with an unaffected sigh. He flicked an invisible speck of dust off his near horse's collar, and looked as though he meant what he said.

"But tell me now, in your turn, why you catechize me like this?" inquired Horace, not without raillery, as his former not very charitable misgivings as to the Prince's own designs upon Georgette recurred to him.

They were not above a hundred yards' distance from the Hôtel Macrobe, and the phaeton was still going like wildfire. The Prince said: "Repeat to me once more what you affirmed about Georgette's blamelessness."

"I do; I affirm her entirely blameless, upon my word," said Horace earnestly.

"Well, then," answered the Prince with gravity, "if Mdlle. Georgette will do me the honour to accept me, I will make her my wife."

Horace looked quickly round, as if his first thought was that the Prince was joking. But M. d'Arcola was perfectly composed. He spoke as if he had just announced his coming marriage to a princess of his own rank.

CHAPTER XV.

A RECOGNITION.

THE Prince's communication ought to have left Horace indifferent, but somehow it did not. Let those explain this who, having ever formed the manly resolution not to love a girl because she was poor, or low-born, or anything else uneligible, find these scruples accounted as nought by others richer, higher, and prouder than themselves. Horace was aware that there was not a living man who would have shrunk more sensitively from a mésalliance than the Prince of Arcola. But, apparently, *his* notions of a mésalliance were not those of the common world.

At dinner, without alluding to the circumstance, Horace asked his wife whether she had yet called on the Pochemolles at their new residence.

"Perhaps it would be civil," said he pensively, "as they sent us a letter, mentioning they were going to move."

"I will call, dear, if you wish it," answered Angélique in her tranquil voice; "but I could not do so before, for they gave no address."

"M. d'Arcola tells me they are at Meudon," said Horace.

"Very wise of them to choose the country," remarked M. Macrobe: "pure air, broad fields, life healthy and cheap."

"And shooting for those who can shoot," chimed in the Crimean hero.

"And shooting, as you say, Captain," assented his uncle.

For some time past it had become a sort of mania with M. Macrobe to depict rural bliss. Virgil never took greater pains to vaunt the charms of a rustic life, the sweet breath of kine, the scent of new-mown hay, and the unadulterated purity of country milk and butter than did the financier. Especially was it good to hear him hold forth on the pride and pomp of a manorial estate, the waving acres, the waggons groaning under loads of storied sheaves, the rows of peasants bowing with glad homage before their lord, and the turreted castle gleaming majestuously in the summer sun over river, field, and wood. Angélique, as if repeating a music lesson, would take up this pastoral in a minor key, saying that she adored the country, and would " so like to have a small castle where they might spend the autumn." Captain Clarimon, not less bucolic, opined that a great noble should slaughter winged fowl on a grandiose scale, organize battues that would muster a whole country side, and run down a stag now and then with accompaniment of horn-tooting to stir up the minds of the clodhoppers.

That was a true saying of the ancients: *Gutta cavat lapidem, non vi, sed sæpe cadendo.* Under the frequency of these Georgic aspersions Horace was imperceptibly beginning to feel that the man who had no landed property, nor horned cattle, nor preserves, had missed the preordained purpose of existence. To be sure, he might have purchased all these things on the very morrow with his wife's dowry had it pleased him. But he did not look upon this money as his. At her marriage M. Macrobe had given his daughter two millions and a half of francs, but Horace had insisted they should stand in Angélique's own name on the books of the Crédit Parisien, and be tied down absolutely to her by contract : and there he meant to leave them, never claiming the privilege of touching a centime. Besides, his notions of an enviable demesne were not associated with a brand-new estate, cut out to order and bought with ready money. When he thought of the matter the towers of Clairefontaine rose vaguely before him— Clairefontaine which might have been his, had his relative Guineaman made his fortune by swindling his contemporaries under the rose, instead of selling them openly in the broad light of day.

"Everybody likes the country," he remarked mechanically, in answer to M. Macrobe's observation.

It was Italian Opera night, and, on leaving the dining-room, Angélique was cloaked in a flowing white *burnous* by the attentive Crimean hero, who was continually and jealously on the watch to render little services. The same warrior brought the opera-glass, and took Angélique's fan into his special custody. He also made himself useful in fastening those six-button gloves which ladies were then inaugurating, and which, had they existed in the time of Job, might have added one more to that sorely-vexed patriarch's trials of patience.

"You will take me to the opera, won't you, Horace?" asked Angélique, helplessly surrendering her small wrists to the gallant Captain.

"Yes, dear," answered Horace with the docility characteristic of husbands during the first year of their marriage; and he inquired what opera it was.

"I think it's *Don Giovanni*."

"Oh dear!" sighed Aunt Dorothée, whose venerable head was crowned with an assortment of limp feathers that gave her the appearance of a demoralized bustard. "That's the play where the stage opens up and swallows a living being in the flames. You'll come away before that happens, won't you, dear? I'm always afraid to see that young man burn his clothes."

"You shall come away when you like, aunt dear," promised Angélique. "Are you ready, Horace?"

Horace was ready, and so was the Captain, who, as in duty bound, offered the Marquise his arm. But as they all sailed out together, with the exception of M. Macrobe, who participated in the belief of M. Alphonse Karr that music is but the most expensive of all noises, a servant announced "Monsieur Emile," and this upset the arrangements. Horace, not over sorry to be reprieved from four hours' stewing in a grand tier box, settled to join his wife later in the evening, the Crimean hero meanwhile undertaking to guard her under his valiant protection.

"The night is so fine that Emile and I will walk down," said Horace; "and I will be with you about the second act."

"And will you come too, Emile?" asked

Angélique a little timidly, for she never brought herself without hesitation to call her grave young brother-in-law by his Christian name.

"I am scarcely in opera attire, sister," he answered kindly. "I only looked in on the chance of finding Horace disengaged, but I blame myself for monopolizing him in this way."

"Oh, you are quite right to come, brother, but you should let us see you oftener, and be here earlier, so as to dine with us."

She said this amiably, glancing up a little to her husband for approval, for she knew it was the surest way to please him to show civility to his brother. Then she held out her tiny hand to Emile, which he shook, thanking her.

"Well, old fellow, it's a long while since we two took an evening walk like this," began Horace, as he and Emile paced together arm-in-arm.

They were in the Champs Elysées, under the crystal dome of a clear sky, blue with the dark-blue of night, and irradiated by a moon of such silvery brightness that it made the gaslights look like dull red dots. Paris shows well on such nights when the trees throw long lace-pattern shadows on the pavements, rows of fair white mansions gleam like polished marble, and lovers stroll in pairs, whispering that *Je t'aime* which is of daily use in none but the " Latin " tongues.

"Do you remember those pleasant walks," continued Horace, "when we first came to Paris, three years ago? It seems like ten years off. We worked all day, often half the night, but now and then we gave ourselves a holiday, and took it out like this, wandering about the streets and guessing at the future. How gay they appeared to me then, the streets; and what smiles I used to see on the faces of the passers-by! Paris always struck me as a perpetual fair. Ah, those were the happy times!"

"But you are happy now, Horace?"

"Oh yes."

And there was a pause.

"But tell me about yourself," added Horace,

breaking off from some internal reflection which had brought a flitting frown to his brow. "Let me look at you—you grow paler and paler. Why do you work so much, eh? Everybody talks of your indefatigableness. A judge told me the other night that if he had worked as you do at his age he would have been a Chief Justice of Appeal by this time."

"Then you see, work does lead to something," smiled Emile.

"Ah, but my judge added the proviso: 'Or I should have been in my coffin,' which didn't reassure me."

"I don't feel as if I were near my coffin, dear fellow. Pale men, like threatened men, live long."

"And you are happy in your way and satisfied?"

"Why should I not be?"

"But you have no ambition, restlessness, eagerness to outpass somebody or do something before the appointed time? I sometimes marvel at your calmness; we don't seem to be moulded out of the same clay."

"I suppose everybody has his small beacon of

ambition beckoning him, Horace, but I fancy the surest way of attaining it is by plainly following the beaten track. It may be the longest road, but cuts across country often lead one into quagmires."

A short silence and then they reached the Rue de Rivoli, that noblest of modern streets, with its half-mile colonnade, forum of foreigners, *Via Sacra* of hotel-keepers. Broughams glanced along the broad highway, bearing muffled forms to theatre and routs. Unbroken lines of flaming jets intensified by dazzling reflectors flooded the arches with light. Spaniards, Americans, Germans, Englishmen sauntered up and down smoking their after-dinner cigars, and examining the accumulated treasures of the shops.

"What wealth!" exclaimed Horace. "Paris has indeed under this reign become Cosmopolis. But, now, I wonder" — and he laughed — "I wonder if all these people we see here, and all the people in the shops there, were suddenly to sit down and say, 'We will make restitution of every franc that we have ever unduly earned,

and of every franc that our fathers before us
unduly earned and bequeathed to us in inheritance;' and supposing some power of another
sphere were to inspire them with the faculty of
making a faultless estimate of these sums—I
wonder, I say, when the balance had been struck,
how many of these persons we behold congregated
from all the corners of the globe would have money
enough left to smoke their cigars, or to keep those
sumptuous shops going."

"What can have put such a thought as that
into your head?" asked Emile, astonished. "This
is disquieting philosophy."

"I was thinking about the nice discussions we
barristers could raise as to what was honest gold
and what was not. Given two men with large
fortunes and relatives to inherit them. The first
has been, say, a wine-merchant, and has conscientiously mixed his wines with logwood and
water for a stated series of years. The second
has with integrity followed a trade, which, during
his lifetime, was lawful, but which was prohibited
later, though even then opinions were divided

respecting it. Now which is the cleaner money of the two: that of the wine-merchant who regaled the public with a purple decoction at fancy prices or that of the other man, who, pursuing a doubtful trade, yet conducted it according to his lights, straightforwardly?"

"I should like to hear more about the doubtful trade," answered Emile, quietly. "There are possibly in this crowd some police-spies from the Prefecture, sent out to worm themselves into the confidence of unsuspecting men, trap them into anti-Bonapartist utterances, and get them transported to Cayenne. As times go, the trade is a lawful one, but I should be sorry to finger any of its profits."

"Naturally. You speak like the good fellow you are. Still, I ask myself how many men would feel bound to do what we have done, and renounce the estate where their fathers lived because it had been bought back after arbitrary confiscation, with the money of a dealer who—well, who did what the custom of those days perfectly sanctioned."

This was the first time since many a long month that Horace so much as alluded to a subject which Emile had dismissed from his own mind once and for all as not admitting of discussion. Emile looked at his brother with an expression in which sudden surprise and dismay were painfully blended, and it was in quite an altered voice that he said: " You are surely not regretting a sacrifice that was made of your own free will, Horace ? "

"Not in the least. No, there's no regret whatever," and Horace laughed again in an off-hand way, though somewhat constrainedly. "To begin with, our father made the sacrifice before us, and I know he would take it so much to heart if either of us abandoned our resolution, that I wouldn't assume the responsibility even if I *had* changed my mind. But I haven't—no—so don't be alarmed. I was only speaking on supposition —supposing there were two other men placed in our predicament, and you and I were commenting on what they ought to do, I think, then, the case might afford scope for argument. That's all."

And argue it they did, walking slowly during two hours through the streets, often retracing their steps, occasionally stopping altogether; the one conversing with animation but simulated unconcern, the other too much troubled to say all he would have said had he felt the debate to be as hypothetical a one as his brother would have had it seem. At eleven they stood outside the Opera House, and the theme was not yet exhausted, for, bidding each other good-night under the portico of the theatre, Horace said, a little flushed but cheerfully: "Mind, old fellow, all this is purely speculative; talk to while away the time and nothing else. It was our walk set me thinking of Clairefontaine. You recollect our visit there; that old woman who shewed us over the place, our ovation when we returned to the worthy town, and the stones with which the good people pelted us in guise of *pax vobiscum* to the railway-station. It was just such a night as this. By-the-way, you hear oftener from Brussels than I do: our father was quite well, at the last writing?"

"Quite well, thank God."

"I will write to him myself in a day or two. But his letters to me are sad; they give one the idea that he is suffering. Well, good-night, dear fellow, and mind what I repeat, this evening's chat has been words, nothing more."

"Good-night, Horace."

They shook hands and parted; but had Horace followed his brother round the corner of the street he would have seen that, collected as Emile had been all the evening, tears started to his eyes as soon as his brother's back was turned, and that he walked home with the lagging step of one who had received a blow, whose faith in a loved being has been shaken.

Horace was conducted by a bustling attendant to the box of Mdme. la Marquise de Clairefontaine. A prima-donna was indulging in terrific screams under pretence of singing, and the audience hung spell-bound on the enchanting sounds. The fig-nosed planter, alone, whom Horace descried slumbering in a pit-tier lodge under the mutely reproachful eye of Mrs. Planter, appeared to protest by his attitude against this manner of spending an evening. Every part of the house was crowded, and the Italian Opera being the only theatre in which the play-going Frenchwoman will unveil her shoulders and the Frenchman submit to the tyranny of swallow-tails, the effect was not bad.

"Do you recognize any one you know?" asked Angélique prettily, making way for Horace on the chair beside her, which the Crimean hero had vacated on his entrance.

Angélique's large, limpid eyes were always so intently fixed when uttering the simplest questions that Horace detected nothing unusually attentive in their gaze on this occasion.

"Let me see, dear child," he said, taking her glass. "On the tier above there's Mdme. de Margauld; is that who you mean? a pretty woman, and dresses sensibly; then there's Mdme. de Masseline, wife of my co-deputy. They say her pin-money comes from the Prefecture, where she carries all that she picks up in society. I refuse to believe it, though, for you ladies malign one another mercilessly, and it was a lady gave me that pretty piece of scandal. Then there's the Austrian ambassadress, and Mdlle. Cora, the dancer, costumed with infinitely more propriety than her Excellency, and Mdme. Gribaud — why, yes, dear child, I recognize everybody. But there's not a face "—restoring the glass and nodding with a smile, "more pretty, or a dress more tasteful than those of someone whose name you may guess."

"Look again," said Angélique, her mild eyes calmly, inquiringly, intent as before. "There, almost opposite us."

Horace looked again, and this time his researches were guided by several pairs of eyes in the stalls converging towards one point, a box where shone a truly imperial beauty. She was the most striking face in the house; but it took Horace some seconds to rally his fluttering impressions and to grasp who it was. Georgette!

"Their coming in caused quite a sensation during the first entr'acte," pursued Angélique quietly; but she never withdrew her eyes from her husband, who now did not put down the glass. "Everybody seems to admire her."

"Reminds me of those Georgian beauties whom I saw at Constantinople; lustrous faces, scarlet lips, and dark hair," struck in the Crimean hero; "but I prefer blonde features."

In spite of himself, Horace's gaze seemed rivetted. The box was occupied by Madame Pochemolle and the draper, but these excellent people, not knowing much of etiquette, had given the place of honour to their daughter. In the background the Prince of Arcola was dimly recognizable. Georgette was pensively rapt in the music, but at intervals she turned to answer some remark of the Prince's, or bent her head with modest grace in token that she was listening to him. Could this be the Georgette of the Rue Ste. Geneviève? Was it possible that a few yards of silk and a trinket or two had been able to convert the humble girl of the linen-shop into a beauty outvying all the most courted women of the chief city of cities? When Horace put down the glass it was with a slight tremor of the hand.

"Is she not beautiful?" said Angélique, in whose voice no unaccustomed inflection was noticeable, at least to her husband.

"Yes—that is, no—I find her altered a little, improved, perhaps," answered Horace, affecting an indifference which his reverie-struck mood belied.

"Good gracious!" dolefully exclaimed Aunt Dorothée, at this opportune juncture. "Here is that dreadful Statue come to take that young man down into the flames. My dear, I was quite unwell last time I saw this."

"Well, madame, we will leave then," said Horace, at once rising. "Angélique, child, shall we go?"

"Yes, dear," she murmured simply, and there was a putting on of cloaks and screwing down of opera-glasses, which called into play the Crimean hero's chivalry, and filled up a minute. During that minute, after assisting in the swathing of his aunt, Horace came to the front of the box and gazed again across the house. His glance may have been charged with something of electricity, for Georgette almost instantly looked up and saw him. But had he been a stranger seen for the first time, had he been one of those curly-pated dandies in the stalls, one of the box-openers in the lobbies, one of the chorus-singers on the stage, her expression could not have been more stony, more coldly unconscious. She turned her head away without vouchsafing a mark of recognition, either unfriendly or the reverse. Horace turned away too, and drew out his handkerchief to wipe away a drop of moisture from his brow. As he did so he observed the cypher on his handkerchief. It was one of those which Georgette had embroidered for him as a gift two years before.

END OF VOL. II.

London: Printed by SMITH, ELDER and Co., 15, Old Bailey, E.C.

www.ingramcontent.com/pod-product-compliance
Lightning Source LLC
Chambersburg PA
CBHW030315240426
43673CB00040B/1170

Royal Pakhoungte takes his readers on a tour de force with a passionate, engaging, and critical reinvestigation of Paul's apostolic suffering from a disability perspective. As a skilled exegete, aided with sociological and rhetorical tools of interpretation, he brings the relevant passages from 2 Corinthians to life from their original social context that stigmatized the disabled bodies. By examining Paul's suffering compounded by his physical disability, Royal successfully exhumes the mostly overlooked liberative theological insights embedded within the text to affirm the dignity of a disabled person. Hence, he invites the church to be the alternate space in the world celebrating the physical differences without hierarchy and stigma. I highly recommend this book for all, both students and theologians.

Roji Thomas George, DTh
Professor of New Testament,
South Asia Institute of Advanced Christian Studies, Bangalore, India

This interesting book focuses on Paul's narration of suffering and weakness in 2 Corinthians from a disability perspective, analysing the mental and psychological pressures that Paul experienced in his life and ministry. The author has developed a disability hermeneutic that critically examines the effect of societal attitudes, which are themselves disabling for a person who is already struggling with physical challenges. His thorough investigation is an important contribution that fills the gap in Pauline scholarship in the area of disability discourse.

Susan Mathew, PhD
Professor of New Testament, Faith Theological Seminary, Manakala, India
Founder-Director of Deepti Special School and Rehabilitation Centre,
Manakala, India